Discovering English with Sketch Engine

a corpus-based approach to language exploration

Workbook and Glossary

James Thomas

Discovering English with Sketch Engine

Workbook & Glossary

March 2016

VERSATILE

Copyright © James Thomas 2016

ISBN 978-80-260-9579-8

All rights reserved.

No part of this publication may be reproduced or transmitted

in any form or by any means, electronic or mechanical,

including photocopying, recording, or any information storage

or retrieval system, without prior permission from the author or publisher.

Cover design

Martin Hrdina

Typesetting

Peter Docherty

Contact

deske@versatile.pub

Discovering English with Sketch Engine

Workbook and Glossary

Using Corpora
to learn English
to learn about English
to learn about learning English

James Thomas

VERSATILE
http://versatile.pub
http://lulu.com/spotlight/versatilepub

V E R S A T I L E

	Introduction	2
Chapter 1	Words and Phrases	6
Chapter 2	Taking Ownership of your Concordance Page	16
Chapter 3	What's on the Menu?	19
Chapter 4	Thesaurus	29
Chapter 5	Top Level Queries continued	31
Chapter 6	It depends on the context	44
Chapter 7	Text Types	54
Chapter 8	Corpus Query Language in detail	63
Chapter 9	Parallel Corpora	73
Chapter 10	Collocation	78
Chapter 11	Word sketches	84
Chapter 12	Word sketch differences	93
Chapter 13	Word list	96
Chapter 14	DIY corpora	101
Chapter 15	Pride and Prejudice	102
	Glossary	104
	Answer Key	117
	Discussion slips	124

Preface

Discovering English with Sketch Engine, or DESKE for short, was first published in the spring of 2015. The second edition was published a year later, along with this accompanying workbook and glossary.

Workbook

The workbook provides readers of the second edition of DESKE with structured spaces in which to make their notes on the approximately 350 corpus research questions that appear throughout the book.

Each chapter also has quiz questions, some with a language focus and some with a linguistic focus. These are mostly multiple-choice and short answer questions and there is an answer key towards the back of the book. Some of the tables and diagrams in DESKE have been reproduced as tasks.

In addition, there are Research and Discussion Questions concerning issues that arise in each chapter. Because DESKE is studied by current and future language teachers, some of these questions are distinctly orientated towards the application of corpora to language pedagogy. In a discussion sense, they benefit from some negotiation. This book provides two approaches:

- they appear in each chapter with some space for note-making
- in classroom situations, teachers can use these questions in milling activities. Photocopiable sets of ten slips for each chapter are provided at the end of this book, where the instructions for conducting the activity can also be found.

Glossary

This book also contains a glossary of terms related to grammar and syntax, vocabulary and semantics, discourse and pragmatics, corpus and general linguistics, and language education.

E-learning

At the time of writing, an e-learning course to support the book is under development. It is being created in Moodle and will contain such things as videos, language learning activities, linguistic terminology activities, discussion forums, a wiki and links to related readings. Watch the Versatile website for news of its progress and launch. It is planned to go online in late 2016 and will be announced on the Versatile website.

Creating this work book with Filemaker

This book and the e-learning course have been prepared using a program created in the database software, Filemaker. Once the questions and answers were entered and categorized, the program generated the GIFT coding which prepared them for exporting to Moodle. It also formatted the questions and answers for printing, more or less as they appear in this book. And it also formatted the slip swapping activities. For more information about this program, see the Versatile website.

Introduction

The Introduction is a longish essay that introduces some of the linguistic and pedagogical pioneers in the use of corpora in language education and contemporary lexicography. It also outlines features of corpora, modes of enquiry as well as some key aspects of language, linguistics and language pedagogy that serve as the foundations for the book. Here are some quiz questions based on the Introduction.

Quiz Questions

Question 1: What does "affordance" mean?

    a. the cost of using proprietary software
    b. the amount of time spent learning something
    c. the multiple learning opportunities that a text offers
    d. using corpora to discover hidden patterns in text

Question 2: What is attested language?

    a. language that is used in making tests
    b. language that has been invented to exemplify some aspect of language
    c. language that has been chosen to exemplify some aspect of language
    d. language that has been produced as a genuine communicative act
    e. none of these

Question 3: What is core language?

    a. it is used for business transactions
    b. it is a dialect spoken and written in and around London
    c. it consists of easy vocabulary and grammar
    d. it is a subset of a language that contains the elements that all idiolects and dialects have in common

Question 4: What is lexicogrammar?

    a. a term created by Halliday.
    b. it expresses the mutual dependence of grammar and vocabulary.
    c. it embraces the lower levels of the Hierarchy of Language, stopping before sentence.
    d. all of these.

Question 5: How do contemporary dictionaries differ from older ones?

    a. modern dictionaries are prescriptive.
    b. modern dictionaries contain information about grammar as well as vocabulary.
    c. modern dictionary definitions are lists of synonyms.
    d. it is not possible to use a modern dictionary without being able to use a corpus.
    e. All modern dictionaries are bilingual.

Question 6: What is Sketch Engine?

    a. SKE is a corpus of many millions of words
    b. SKE is a grammar and dictionary all in one website
    c. SKE is an American company
    d. SKE is draws sketches of words that look like pictures
    e. SKE is a tool used by applied linguists to analyse language, and by teachers and students to explore and exploit language patterns

Question 7: Which contexts do words occur in?

    a. in the context of other words
    b. in the context of grammatical relationships
    c. in the context of people communicating
    d. all of these options

Question 8: Does a reference corpus aim to represent everything it can about a language?

    a. Yes
    b. No

Question 9: What is an armchair linguist?

    a. most Neo-Firthian linguists are armchair linguists
    b. linguists who rely on intuition
    c. philosophers who sit in deep soft comfortable armchairs
    d. armchair linguists barely exist anymore

Question 10: Where do our idiolects come from?

    a. from our family and friends
    b. from our interaction with people
    c. from our exposure to the media
    d. from our education
    e. all of these options

Question 11: Who cleans up the language in corpora so that there are no mistakes or taboo language?

    a. nobody cleans it up
    b. the language police
    c. the Association for Pure English
    d. corpus builders

Question 12: **Why aren't corpora commonly used in language classrooms?**

    a. few teachers can use them
    b. they are considered time-consuming
    c. they are more suited to a pattern- based view of language than a rule-based one
    d. few teachers have lexicogrammar view of language
    e. all of these options

Question 13: **Why is fuzziness important in language study?**

    a. questions have more than one answer
    b. learners need to accept that language is a probabilistic
    c. the answer to many language questions start with *it depends*
    d. students need to be willing to experiment with the language when producing it
    e. all of these options

Question 14: **What higher order thinking skills (HOTS) are involved in corpus use by language learners?**

    a. using corpora involves formulating appropriate search questions
    b. language data has to be interpreted critically
    c. learners create new knowledge for themselves as they turn data into information and then knowledge
    d. all of these options

Research and Discussion Questions

A. How can language be considered data?

B. How do you understand Firth's widely quoted claim?

    You shall know a word by the company it keeps.

C. What do you understand by Stubbs' statement, and is it related to Firth's "company" claim?

D. It is not the words which tell you the meaning of the phrase, but the phrase which tells you the meaning of the individual words in it. What do you think is meant by:

    Halliday describes language not in terms of rules, but as sets of systems that involve choices made according to describable criteria: Language is "a network of systems, or interrelated sets of options for making meaning".

E. Language teaching talks a lot about rules. Do you think Halliday has something valuable to contribute to this?

F. What are some pros and cons of using attested language as teaching examples?

G. What do you understand by the term, the Flipped Classroom?

Discussion Notes

Chapter 1 Words and Phrases

This chapter introduces the main search field for creating queries in Sketch Engine. In the process, the foundations are laid for answering language questions through interpreting the data that is returned from the Simple Query search field.

The notions of pattern of normal usage, frequency and probability are key to answering questions about word meaning, grammatical relationships and genre appropriacy.

An essential, underlying principle in learning, is knowledge creation. The first task here is to reconstruct this diagram that appears in the Preface of the book.

Use the words information, knowledge and data. And make a brief statement about each of them.

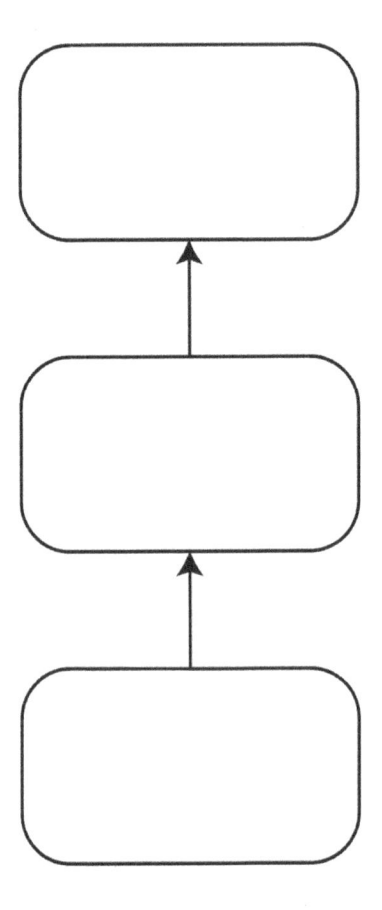

The Questions from DESKE

The space under each question is intended for brief notes on your corpus findings.

Question 1   Does *whose* only refer to people or does it also refer to non-living things?

Question 2   Do we say *people who* or *people that*?

Question 3   How is the idiom *kick the bucket* used?

Question 4   Do *problems lie*? If so, what is meant by this?

Question 5   Do people respond to something with the phrase *that's a moot point* to mean that they don't believe what was just said?

Question 6   Can you say *handsome woman* in English?

Question 7   Does anyone really say *while holidaying*?

Question 8   Would you expect each of the *go* troponyms to be less frequent than the one to the left of it?

Question 9   Would you expect that these frequencies impact on the order in which native speaker children acquire them, or learners learn them?

Question 10   *One swallow does not a summer make.* What is this curious word order?

Question 11   Is *open door* an adjective + noun or a verb + noun? Or something else?

Question 12   I've come across *boldly go* a few times and wondered if it is more than a collocation.

Question 13   In the Introduction, someone was said to *sleep furiously*. Where did this counter-intuitive description of sleeping come from?

Question 14   I've heard the phrase, *Just when you thought it was safe to …* and I wonder how it might be used. Is it ironic?

Question 15   I've also heard *in my point of view*. I thought it was *from*...

Question 16   How is the word *germane* used?

Question 17   What other words and phrases has English borrowed?

Question 18   When might one use *curiouser* instead of *more curious*?

Question 19   Is *Pacific Ocean* written with this capitalisation?

Question 20   Is *Internet* written with this capitalisation?

Question 21   Does the phrase *who'd have thought* stand alone? Or is it a part of a sentence? If so, how is it followed up?

Question 22   Is it the norm to use apostrophes with decades?

Question 23   Is it true that English never uses a preposition to end a sentence with?

Question 24   Is *why* followed by both *can't* and *cannot*?

Question 25   Are wh- words followed by both *can't* and *cannot*?

Question 26   Is the spelling of words with either –ise or -ize a difference between UK and US English?

Question 27   Do you love me …

Question 28   'What's the difference between …?'

Question 29   What is your favo*rite …

Question 30   What do we do with words like *thingamabob*?

Question 31   What is the pattern that *cahoots* operates in?

Question 32   How *ecstatic* is life in London?

Question 33   What wayward items might appear in the BNC?

Question 34   Did *tweet* meaning something before the social medium, Twitter?

Question 35   How do company names compare in the BNC and the NMC?

Quiz Questions: Language

Question 1:   **What company does *kick the bucket* keep in the BNC?**
   a. fall down drunk
   b. die
   c. racing
   d. struggle
   e. in the garden

Question 2: The collocation *handsome woman* is used to describe a certain type of woman in modern English.

    a. True
    b. False

Question 3: What is the modern English equivalent of *doth*?

Question 4: Is *why* followed by both *can't* and *cannot*?

    a. *why can't* and *why cannot* are standard constructions
    b. *why can't* is standard, but *why cannot* is rare
    c. *why can't* is rare, but *why cannot* is standard

Question 5: When someone is *in cahoots with* someone, ...

    a. marriage is in the air
    b. they are doing something bad together
    c. they are relatives
    d. they are making a lot of noise

Quiz Questions: Linguistics

Question 1: Why are corpus finds normalised?

    a. because they are easy to compute
    b. so that non-specialists can understand them more easily
    c. so that findings can be compared across various corpora
    d. they aren't

Question 2: Deviations from the normal, standard, typical way of doing something are said to be ....

    a. open choice
    b. marked choice
    c. errors
    d. unattested language

Question 3: Match the terms with their definitions

polysemy	a word which is at a lower semantic level
troponym	a verb which is a sub-type of another superordinate verb
hyponym	words which are sub of the same superordinate
co-hyponym	a word which is at a higher semantic level
hypernym	when a word has several meanings

Question 4: **Why is a corpus more suitable for language study than the whole internet?**

a. the texts in corpora have been selected according to guiding principles
b. corpora are samples of language
c. corpus tools permit the processing of language
d. the web reveals what is possible whereas a corpus reveals what is probable
e. all of these reasons

Question 5: **What does *grammaticality* refer to?**

a. a sentence with no grammar mistakes has this
b. a nonsense sentence that is grammatically acceptable
c. when a sentence has been made up to teach a grammar point
d. an intuitive judgement about the accuracy of a sentence

Blooms Taxonomy

In terms of the level of activity expected of students, this mid-20th century hierarchy has influenced the design of courses and materials extensively. Write the six levels into this diagram, starting with the most basic level of activity, remembering. The others are creating, analysing, applying, understanding and evaluating.

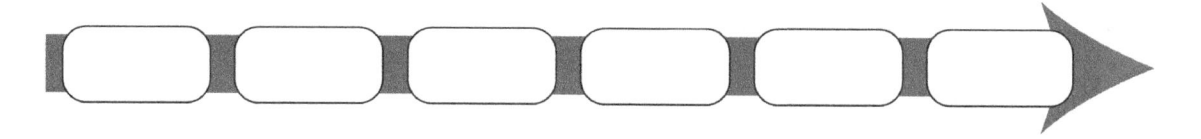

In thinking about language teaching, the relationships between the four skills and four systems need to borne in mind. For example, which of the four systems are invoked in reading?

Draw lines connecting the skills and systems, showing these relationships.

Vocabulary   Reading

Grammar   Writing

Phonology   Speaking

Functions   Listening

Research and Discussion Questions

A. What do you think Kilgarriff meant when he said, *Language is never ever, ever, random*? What is its significance to language teaching and learning?

B. What do you think the relationship is between a word's frequency and it being acquired by native speakers and by learners? (Q.9)

C. When might you use *curiouser* instead of *more curious*?

D. How do spelling mistakes get into corpora? How should corpus-users deal with them?

E. In Q. 4 some "quirky collocations" are listed. Which of them are worth knowing for (a) receptive purposes and (b) productive purposes? Why do you think so?

F. Are you aware of any lexical gaps in English? For example, there may be words in another language you know which do not have equivalents in English.

Discussion Notes

Chapter 2   Taking Ownership of your Concordance Page

This short chapter teaches Sketch Engine users how to customise aspects of the interface. This is no cosmetic operation, rather adjustments to the interface change one's perspectives of the data that is returned after a search. As well, the interface settings influence what can actually be done with the data.

Questions from DESKE

Question 36   What do we take ownership of nowadays?

Question 37   Which structures of *give* are most frequent in which register?

Question 38   Is *moot point* genre-specific?

Hierarchy of Language

Position these terms in the hierarchy: word, phrase, sentence, clause, morpheme, letter, text.

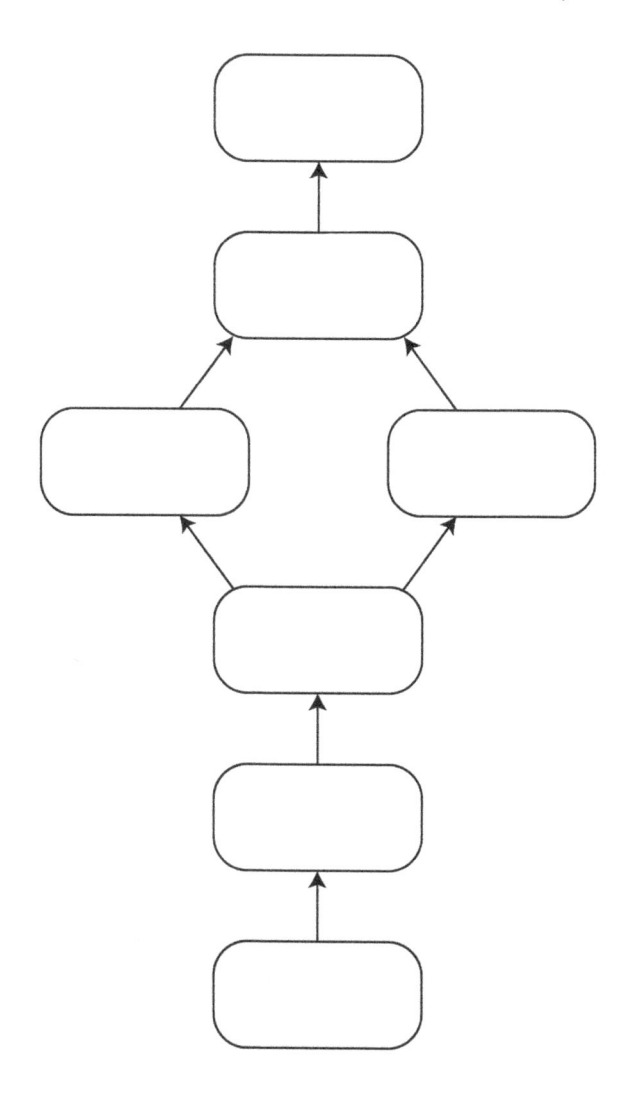

Research and Discussion Question

A. Describe several steps you to to take ownership of your concordance page? What difference do they make to the data you observe.

B. The Hierarchy of Language is a valuable way of viewing the constituents of language with top-down and bottom-up perspectives. Its structure also allows us to posit the upper and lower levels of grammar.

Discussion Notes

Chapter 3 What's on the Menu?

Because the left panel's main menu contains some of the most important controls available for processing corpus data, this chapter introduces them in some detail with many examples of how they can be used in the process of converting data into information. In order to appreciate their value, some aspects of linguistics are introduced. Some rather interesting aspects of language emerge along the way.

Questions from DESKE

Question 39   What things are said to be *unthinkable*?

Question 40   Is *whatsoever* typically used in negative contexts?

Question 41   In the name of language observation, what can we discover about the word *hamper* from a left sort?

Question 42   What words in the context of *hamper* as a noun indicate a different meaning from the verb form of the word?

Question 43   Do marriages break *up* or *down*?

Question 44   Where do English people *go out to*?

Question 45   Why does *wont* return so many concordance lines?

Question 46   Are the BNC's references to the Irish political situation spelled with one capital T or two?

Question 47   In which text types are *The Troubles* discussed?

Question 48   Is *open* typically a verb or adjective with *door* in fiction?

Question 49   Does *be bound to* refer to anything else than something like 'being tied with rope'?

Question 50   I've heard people say that they *are open to* various things. Any things at all?

Question 51   Does *at all* reinforce both positive and negative things? And where in the sentence is it typically found?

Question 52   Does *put* typically have the structure: someone puts something somewhere?

Question 53   Do we prefer *turkey breast* to *breast of turkey*?

Question 54   How often does *Ireland* occur in the context of *the troubles*?

Question 55   Since when has *The Troubles* been a reference to a period in Irish history?

Question 56   How do sentences start with a word like *Given*?

Question 57 Is *Given that* looking back to what has already been said, or forward to what is going to be said?

Question 58 What patterns do other adjectives like *unthinkable* work in?

Question 59 How does the collocation *problem lie* work?

Question 60 How does *arresting officer* come to have more than one meaning?

Question 61 Is the phrase *a long way* complete? Does it occur at the end of an information unit?

Question 62 According to everyone, *according to me* is wrong. Is it? According to whom?

Question 63 Is *thereby* always followed by –ing forms?

Question 64   How context-sensitive are POS tags?

Question 65   I thought *lend* was the verb and *loan* was the noun.

Question 66   What is the difference between *be interested* and *be interesting*?

Question 67   Is *friend* used as a verb?

Question 68   Is *will* a lexical verb in addition to being a marker of futurity?

Question 69   Does Penn Treebank distinguish between *to* as a preposition and as a particle marking the infinitive?

Question 70   Are the typical subjects of *couldn't bear to* nouns or pronouns?

Question 71   Who apart from journalists *pry*?

Question 72   Is *pry* only followed by *into*?

Question 73   What does *pry* into express that similar expressions do not?

Question 74   *Pack of*? When *pack* is not a short form of *packet*, what are the most common things that come in packs?

Question 75   Which words employ meaning-laden suffixes, such as *–cide, -phobia, -proof*?

Question 76   What are the differences between the prefixes *anti* and *ante*?

Question 77   *Harmony* is mostly a technical term in music. How do we use it elsewhere?

Question 78   *Blench* may seem like a perfectly normal English word, but one does not come across it very often. Any comments?

Question 79   What roles do verbs and adjectives play with nouns?

Question 80   Would you consider *well within* a collocation?

Question 81   Compare the distributions of *frame* and other words that also occur with a similar frequency.

Quiz Questions: Language

Question 1:   **Does the verb *hamper* appear to have positive or negative prosody? Write one word.**

   a. positive
   b. negative

Question 2:   **In the BNC, which use of *bound to* is the most frequent?**

   a. chemical bonding
   b. tied with rope or string
   c. emotionally tied
   d. as a modal verb

Question 3:   **Which use of *given that* is anaphoric?**

   a. *that* refers to something which will mentioned later in the same sentence
   b. *that* is pronounced with a reduced vowel
   c. *that* is stressed in speech and marked with a comma in writing

Question 4:   **I thought *lend* was the verb and *loan* was the noun. Which statement accords with your corpus findings?**

   a. both are used as verbs with similar normalised frequencies in the BNC and in ETT
   b. *loan* is far more significant as a verb in ETT than in BNC

Question 5:   **Which collocations in Q.79 make positive semantic prosody?**

   a. avid, dulcet
   b. abject, sheer, wreak
   c. prick up, abiding, sheer
   d. pique, ally, hold down

Quiz Questions: Linguistics

Question 1: **Which one of these features are true of copular verbs?**

a. they are transitive
b. instead of objects they have complements
c. they are generally low frequency verbs
d. their complements can only be nouns

Question 2: **Does Penn Treebank distinguish between *to* as a preposition and as a particle marking the infinitive?**

a. Yes
b. No

Question 3: **Which statement about collocation and colligation is not correct?**

a. collocation is the combination of lexical words
b. colligation is the the combination of a lexical word and its grammatical company
c. collocation refers to sets of related words that occur in a text
d. before 1957 when Firth published his work on collocation and colligation, speakers used language in a much more random way
e. native speakers acquire collocation and colligations of words through exposure

Question 4: **Why do frequency graphs almost always show that some findings are very frequent, with other results becoming less and less frequent?**

Research and Discussion Questions

A. The first of Hoey's ten priming hypotheses (2005:13) reads:

> Every word is primed to occur with particular other words; these are its collocates.

B. Given that our corpus studies support this hypothesis fairly convincingly, how does this impact on our teaching of vocabulary?

C. Question 62 reads: Who decides what is right and wrong? Where do rules come from?

> Cambridge Dictionaries Online has a usage note about *according to me*. Where do they get their authority from? What is the difference between their authority and anybody else's?

> These are important questions for language teachers who constantly deal with right and wrong and the shades in between. Is it necessary to think fuzzy?

D. What is your view?

E. Why might you teach the word *wont* (Question 45)? Who would you be likely to teach it to? What might motivate you to teach it?

> What information about the word would you teach for receptive purposes and for productive purposes?

F. Investigating *unthinkable*:

- What did you find when investigating unthinkable? (Question 39)
- What can you say about an adjective that is not followed by nouns?
- Why are time references salient in the context of *unthinkable*?
- What verbs are common with this adjective?
- How do you account for **the unthinkable**?
- Comment on its morphology. (See also Question 58)

Discussion Notes

Chapter 4   Thesaurus

Sketch Engine's distributional thesaurus is a relatively straightforward tool to use and produces valuable data for vocabulary study. Some of the algorithms that produce this data are used in other Sketch Engine tools that we meet later in DESKE.

Questions from DESKE

Question 82   What semantic relationships hold between a hypernym and the words in the Thesaurus list?

Question 83   What words are listed when you search for a hypernym, e.g. *blue*?

Question 84   How does the data reflect different meanings of polysemous words?

Question 85   What are some adjectives suitable for giving students feedback?

Quiz Questions

Question 1: What is the node word of the word cloud on p.71?

Question 2: Which one of these is not true of a thesaurus?

a. words appear under different headings
b. it is a book of semantically related words
c. entries are arranged in alphabetical order
d. a thesaurus does not contain definitions

Question 3: What is an and/or relationship?

a. when pairs of words are joined by either *and* or *or*
b. when pairs of words are optional
c. when words have either a grammatical or a semantic relationship

Question 4: Which definition of *phrase* given on p.81 corresponds to Sketch Engine's Phrase field?

a. an idiomatic expression
b. a group of words forming part of a clause
c. a syntactic structure without a subject-predicate
d. a string of word forms

Question 5: What term is used for spoken sentences?

Chapter 5   Top Level Queries continued

All of the questions posed so far have been entered in the Simple Query field. In this chapter we meet the other entry fields that facilitate more specific searches. In order to appreciate their utility, a considerable amount of linguistics is introduced in this chapter. Once again, a wide range of new language questions can be asked. This is one of the biggest chapters in this book.

Questions from DESKE

Question 86   Does the asterisk operator yield inflected forms as well as derivations?

Question 87   How can a word family be derived from a corpus?

Question 88   Are these words forms of classical nouns used in the singular or plural?

Question 89   Which words that end in *–sis* form their plural with *–ses*?

Question 90   What are the plural forms of Germanic irregular English nouns?

Question 91   Are possessive forms of English nouns included in the list of word forms of a lemma search?

Question 92   Is *holiday* used as a verb more today than in the BNC days?

Question 93   What do you notice about the company that *grant* and *Grant* or *centre* and *Centre* keep in the BNC?

Question 94   If you are not familiar with the common noun, *thatcher*, can you infer its meaning from multiple contexts?

Question 95   What observations can we make about the word *slouch*?

Question 96   Do we *elaborate* something, or *elaborate* on/about/over something?

Question 97   Is there anything noteworthy about parts of the body used as verbs?

Question 98   Do only people *lope, meander, tread* and *mince*?

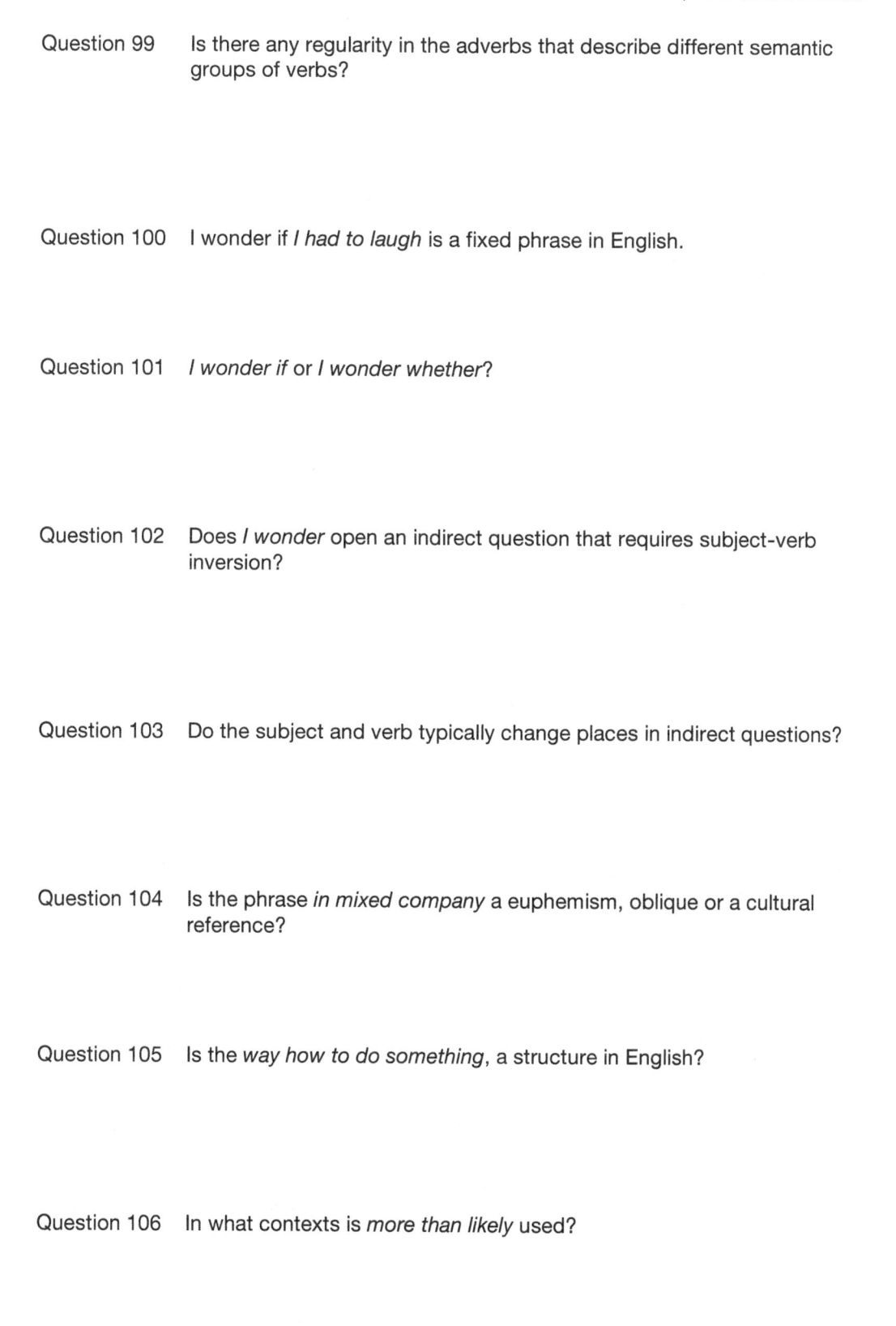

Question 99   Is there any regularity in the adverbs that describe different semantic groups of verbs?

Question 100   I wonder if *I had to laugh* is a fixed phrase in English.

Question 101   *I wonder if* or *I wonder whether*?

Question 102   Does *I wonder* open an indirect question that requires subject-verb inversion?

Question 103   Do the subject and verb typically change places in indirect questions?

Question 104   Is the phrase *in mixed company* a euphemism, oblique or a cultural reference?

Question 105   Is the *way how to do something*, a structure in English?

Question 106   In what contexts is *more than likely* used?

Question 107   Can we say *more than unlikely*?

Question 108   Does the phrase *once in a lifetime* function as an adjective?

Question 109   How do we use the chunks we acquire?

Question 110   What happens after a sentence stem?

Question 111   How different are the words *hair* and *hairs* in English?

Question 112   Are both *though* and *although* used to start sentences? Equally?

Question 113   Is it true that *and* and *but* cannot start sentences?

Question 114   Which is the correct form of these discourse markers when listing things in prose, *first* or *firstly*?

Question 115   Have you ever wondered if some surnames are also common nouns?

Question 116   Are the quantity nouns that follow *of* in the singular or plural?

Question 117   Are singular nouns always used with a determiner? Do they have singular verb agreement?

Question 118   How much information typically appears in brackets (parentheses)?

Question 119   How early did people have email addresses?

Question 120   How is the at symbol used when not in email addresses?

Question 121   Are capital letters used after colons and semicolons?

Question 122   How do answers begin?

Question 123   Which of these *faux* words were in use in the late 20th century?

Question 124   What are some words with the suffix –*ity* indicating the state or quality of the adjective it is attached to?

Question 125   Is *dis*- the only prefix taken by *cover*, as in the title of this book?

Question 126   How do other prefixes fare?

Question 127   Given that Megan is a fairly uncommon name, how did it get such a high score?

Question 128   Are there any affixes making verb forms out of *friend*?

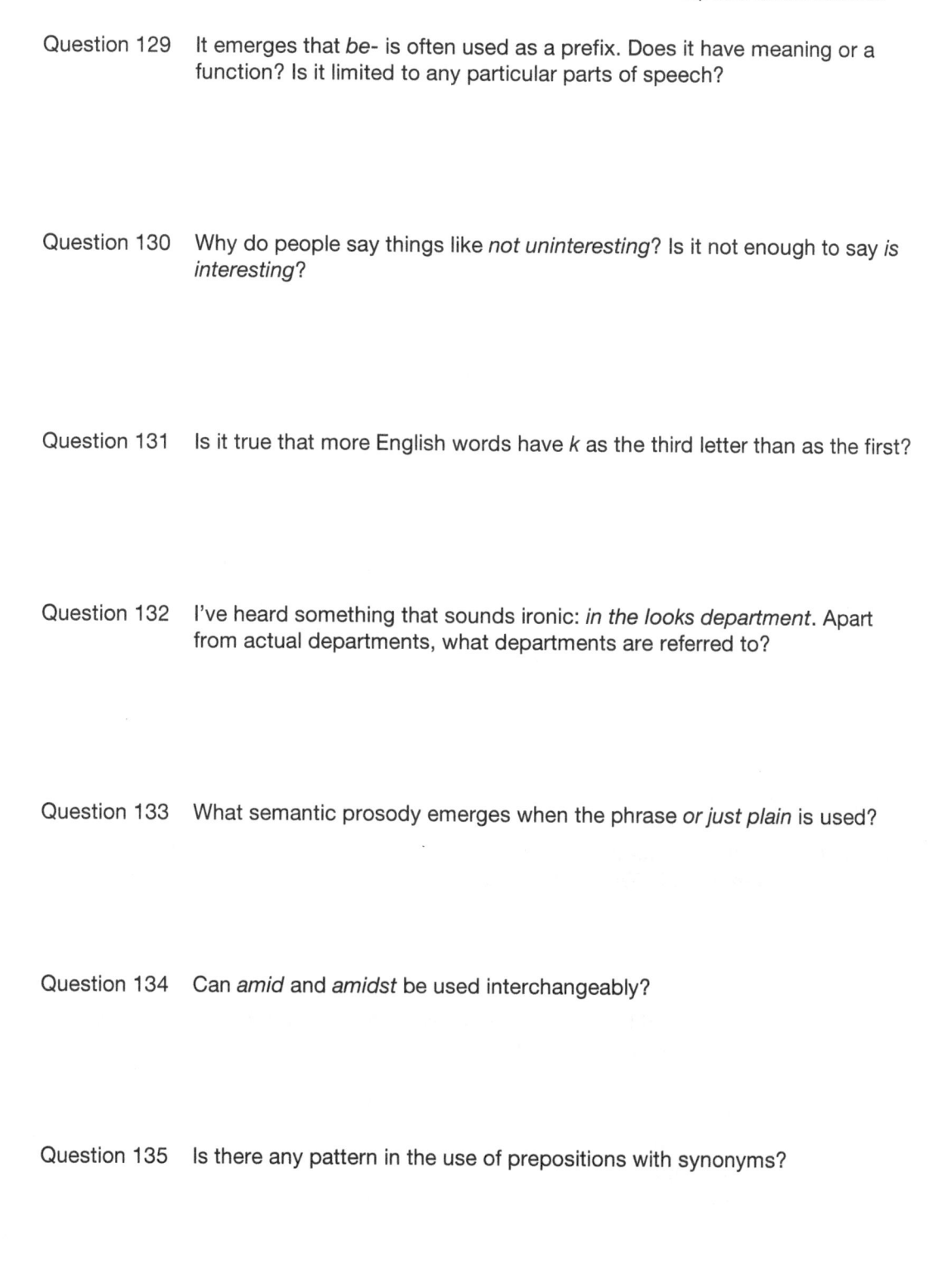

Question 129   It emerges that *be-* is often used as a prefix. Does it have meaning or a function? Is it limited to any particular parts of speech?

Question 130   Why do people say things like *not uninteresting*? Is it not enough to say *is interesting*?

Question 131   Is it true that more English words have *k* as the third letter than as the first?

Question 132   I've heard something that sounds ironic: *in the looks department*. Apart from actual departments, what departments are referred to?

Question 133   What semantic prosody emerges when the phrase *or just plain* is used?

Question 134   Can *amid* and *amidst* be used interchangeably?

Question 135   Is there any pattern in the use of prepositions with synonyms?

Question 136 Can the vertical bar be used to look up British and American spellings at the same time?

Question 137 How many sentences are there in a corpus?

Question 138 Does English permit numbers at the beginning of sentences?

Question 139 Is it true that past participles are only used in compound forms?

Quiz Questions: Language

Question 1: Do the frequencies of the words in the word family of *advantage* demonstrate Zipfian tendencies?

a. Yes
b. No

Question 2: Which one of these features of a word can you not reliably infer from meeting it once in context?

a. its part of speech
b. collocation
c. colligation
d. meaning
e. register

Question 3: Match the verbs on the left with their objects.

shoulder	idea
toe	line
stomach	ride
thumb	(no object)
knuckle	burden

Question 4: Which one of these verbs collocates with *eggshells* and *carefully*?

a. lope
b. meander
c. tread
d. mince

Question 5: Which is the most frequent wording of the most frequent finding in Q.103 (corpus ex.65)

a. Do you know what I think
b. Do you know what I mean
c. Do you know what I thought
d. Do you know what he did

Question 6: What semantic prosody emerges when the phrase *or just plain* is used?

a. clearly positive
b. clearly negative
c. neither positive nor negative
d. sweet, adorable, cute
e. afraid, reluctant, ashamed

Question 7: What can be inferred about the meaning and/or use of *slouch* (noun)?

a. a man of good character
b. a woman of dubious character
c. a man who tends to be lazy and indifferent
d. a man or a woman wearing a particular type of hat
e. people are not usually describe as *a slouch*, only as *no slouch*

Question 8: Which of the forms of perfect are formed with *have*?

a. present perfect
b. past perfect
c. future perfect
d. present perfect passive
e. all of these

Question 9: Match these nouns with their types.

collective	freedom, perseverance, talent
singular	rain, penchant, zodiac, motherland, ethos
mass	jury, minority, headquarters, mafia
uncountable	yeast, lager, muslin, lava, lipstick
abstract	advice, progress, work, hair, rice

Question 10: What semantic prosody emerges when *amid* is used?

a. clearly positive
b. clearly negative
c. neither positive nor negative
d. somewhat negative
e. somewhat positive

Quiz Questions: Linguistics

Question 1: Match these terms with their glosses.

lemma	the smallest unit that expresses a meaning
lexeme	a word or MWU that expresses a single meaning
morpheme	the change of part of speech of a word without inflection
conversion	a process that creates new meanings
word formation	head word for a set of inflections with the same meaning

Question 2: Which term is different from the other three?

a. zero affixation
b. conversion
c. polysemy
d. zero derivation

Question 3: Is it unusual for phrasal verbs to be polyemous?

a. Yes
b. No

Question 4: What do polysemy and homonymy always have in common?

a. the different uses of a word have the same pronunciation
b. the word has the same spelling regardless of meanings
c. the meanings are related
d. the meanings are unrelated

Question 5: Based on BNC data, would you recommend using capital letters after semicolons?

a. Yes
b. No

Question 6: Which of these features are expressed periphrastically in English?

a. the use of the definite article
b. suffixes for comparative and superlative
c. using auxiliary verbs to form aspect
d. choosing a multi-word unit over a single word equivalent

Question 7: How is the sentence stem, *having said that*, used?

a. to lead into more information about what was just said
b. to warn the listener that the next piece of information presents a different perspective
c. to make sure the listener is convinced of what was just said
d. to tell the listener that the speaker does not want to be contradicted

Complete this diagram with the resulting verb-forms and sentence types.

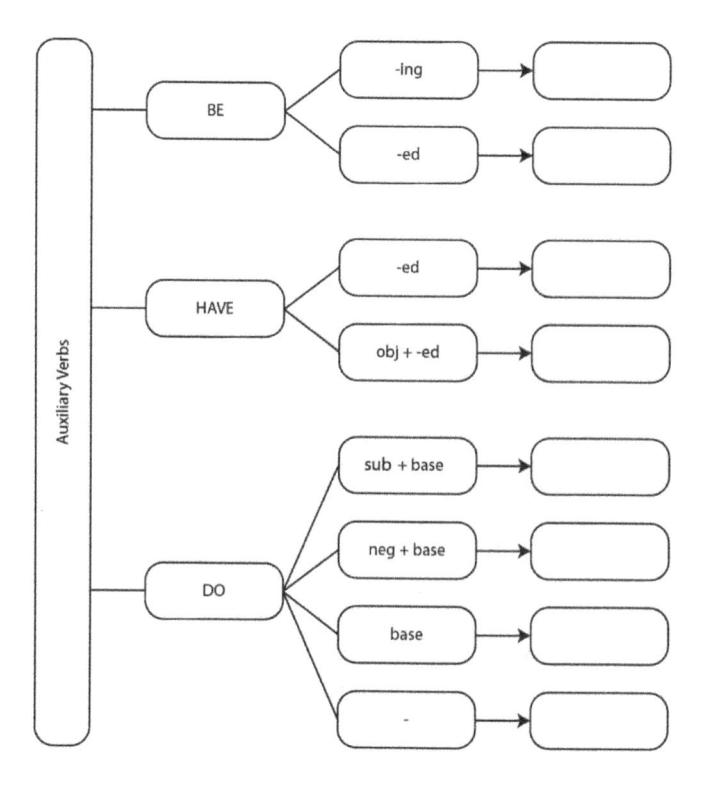

Auxiliary Verbs
- BE
  - -ing → ☐
  - -ed → ☐
- HAVE
  - -ed → ☐
  - obj + -ed → ☐
- DO
  - sub + base → ☐
  - neg + base → ☐
  - base → ☐
  - - → ☐

Research and Discussion Questions

A. What did you find out about the use of numbers at the beginning of sentences? (Q.138)

B. How does knowing a word family thoroughly contribute to fluency? Can you think of any examples? Give some thought to what contributes to dysfluency.

C. The body internal motion verbs in Q.99 each embrace several layers of meaning. This makes them difficult to find good equivalents in another language. What are your thoughts about this?

D. Choose a chunk from Q.109 and report your findings about its text types, the lexical and grammatical company it keeps, and any other observations you make seeing it in multiple contexts. Use the BNC.

E. It often happens that a concept requires a multi-word expression to name it in one language, whereas a single word names it in another language. Would you say that the need for an MWU indicates a lexical gap?

Discussion Notes

Chapter 6 It depends on the context

The middle section of the queries interface enables constraining any search in the top section by other lemmas and/or parts of speech. These contextual options extend searching to a wide range of lexical compounds such as phrasal verbs and collocation in general, as well as to grammatical combinations such as words with prepositions.

Questions from DESKE

Question 140   Is *seize control* a fixed phrase?

Question 141   Is there a standard order in which we say the three items of cutlery?

Question 142   Does *only* at the beginning of a clause predict the emphatic *do*?

Question 143   Do sentence structures have their own meanings or semantics?

Question 144   Is the phrasal verb *put down* separable?

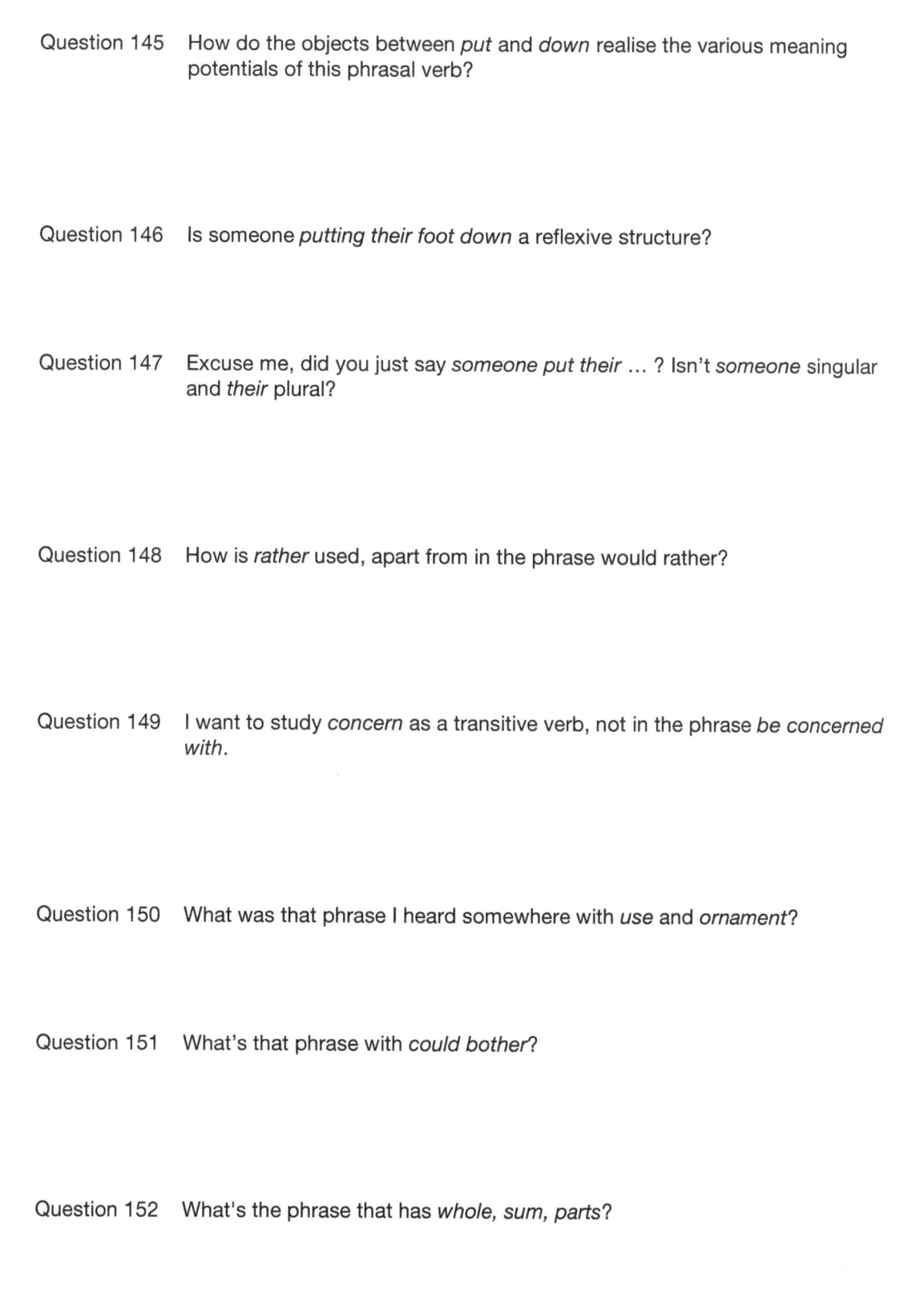

Question 145   How do the objects between *put* and *down* realise the various meaning potentials of this phrasal verb?

Question 146   Is someone *putting their foot down* a reflexive structure?

Question 147   Excuse me, did you just say *someone put their* … ? Isn't *someone* singular and *their* plural?

Question 148   How is *rather* used, apart from in the phrase would rather?

Question 149   I want to study *concern* as a transitive verb, not in the phrase *be concerned with*.

Question 150   What was that phrase I heard somewhere with *use* and *ornament*?

Question 151   What's that phrase with *could bother*?

Question 152   What's the phrase that has *whole, sum, parts*?

Question 153   Does the collocation *catch virus* apply to computer viruses?

Question 154   Is *not only* always completed with *but also*?

Question 155   How do we *elaborate*?

Question 156   Is *up* necessary in the structure with *look* and *dictionary*?

Question 157   What other words would you use to find more examples of this type of fronting?

Question 158   Which two-syllable adjectives form their comparatives with *more*?

Question 159   How productive is the suffix –er with nouns?

Question 160   *Think big*! Shouldn't an adverb complement a verb?

Question 161   When is a passive structure used to convey active meaning?

Question 162   What structures follow *be said*?

Question 163   It would be reasonable to expect the words that follow *positively* to be positive, would it not?

Question 164   What verbs are used in the context of *word* with *dictionary*?

Question 165   What are some features of delexical verbs?

Question 166   What differences can you identify between delexical structures and their single word 'equivalents'?

Question 167   What adjectives are used before the nouns in delexical verb structures?

Question 168   Can you identify any differences between *take a look* and *have a look*?

Question 169   Do any of the words preceding the nouns form compound nouns with them?

Question 170   Is choosing a delexical verb structure over a single verb structure a matter of stylistic variation?

Question 171   Is *having a liking for* something the same as *liking* something?

Question 172   What is the relationship between *dwelling* and *house* in these sentences?

Question 173   Does *include ... such as ...* also find hyponyms in context?

Question 174   What things come under the umbrella of *device* nowadays?

Question 175   What similarities and differences emerge from the bundles of similar words?

Question 176   What company does *join* keep?

Question 177   Who or what *blows their top* and why?

Quiz Questions: Language

Question 1:   **Which pronoun is used for non-sexist 3rd person singular reference? (nominative)**

Question 2:   **Which one of these things is not described as *positively dangerous* in the BNC?**

    a. people
    b. situations
    c. events
    d. weather

Question 3:   **Which of the following qualify as delexical verbs?**

    a. take sb up on an offer
    b. take off
    c. take a bath
    d. take into consideration
    e. take time to

Question 4:   **There are not very many adjectives between *give* and *nod*: what do they express?**

    a. the nod was long and slow
    b. the nod didn't take long
    c. the nod indicated arrogance
    d. the nod was given to a lot of people at once
    e. the nod was promised to occur at a later date

Quiz Questions: Linguistics

Question 1: What does Hanks mean by meaning potential?

   a. it's up to the reader/listener to decide which meaning they'd like a word to have
   b. a word has been invented but no-one has yet decided what it should mean
   c. a word means one thing to some people and something else to other people
   d. of the several meanings a word might have, it is the context which realises or actualises the meaning

Question 2: What are word association lists?

   a. each word in a list is related to the stimulus word in people's minds
   b. an indication of how a group of people feel about a word
   c. fairly predictable
   d. all of these options

Question 3: Are word association lists another way of deriving collocation lists?

   a. Yes
   b. No

Question 4: When positively + adj occur as a collocation, are they usually ...?

   a. an attribute
   b. a predicate

Question 5: What is a "light" verb?

   a. a verb that doesn't carry much meaning
   b. another term for regular verb
   c. one that refers to (shines a light on) another verb
   d. one that has no troponyms

Question 6: Lexical bundles are more closely associated with M language than O language (in LUG terms).

   a. True
   b. False

Question 7: Which of the following are features of bundles?

   a. a bundle typically contains from 2 to 8 words
   b. bundles can include lemmas and part of speech tags
   c. bundles are a very useful format for learners' vocabulary study
   d. bundles form a syntactic unit
   e. None of these

Question 8: Which parts of speech have patterns in the COBUILD sense?

    a. verbs
    b. verbs and nouns
    c. verbs and nouns and adjectives
    d. verbs and nouns and adjectives and adverbs
    e. all parts of speech

Question 9: In the various definitions of verb patterns, which one does not include the subject of the verb?

    a. COBUILD patterns
    b. Hanks' patterns
    c. Word Templates

Question 10: Observing vocabulary in word templates teaches a word's typical company.

    a. True
    b. False

Question 11: What can grammatizing a word template involve?

    a. adding articles and other determiners relevant to the discourse
    b. adding particles that express aspect
    c. declining the noun phrase and conjugating the verb phrase
    d. adding modality
    e. all of these

Question 12: How do word templates teach syntax?

    a. they don't
    b. they are used for jumbled sentence activities
    c. their elements are presented in unmarked word order
    d. the process of grammatising them is part of their presentation

Research and Discussion Questions

A. What observations have you made about the phrasal verb *put down*, in particular about the relationships between it lexical and grammatical contexts?

B. How long has *their/them* been used as non-gender specific 3rd person singular reference?

C. Choose three incomplete phrases from the list in Q.151 and give (a) their complete forms and (b) some usage notes.

D. Can you suggest any better rules or guidelines for adding *-er* and *-est* to adjectives than the one in the first paragraph of Q.158?

E. Compare the hyponyms of *device* in 20th century corpora with 21st century corpora.

F. Compare the bundles of two of the words suggested in Q.175 and describe your findings.

G. How do Hanks' patterns realise the meaning potential of polysemous verbs? In other words, what is included in a pattern that expresses a particular meaning of a verb?

H. If lexical bundles express O language and word templates express M language, what aspects of running text still have to be accounted for?

I. Compare what is learnt about *blow one's top* from the process of creating its word template(s), with what is learnt from a dictionary entry for the idiom.

J. Teaching delexical verbs: what features are worth teaching? How might you introduce delexical verbs to a B2 class? Would their language be more FASI if they used them? Would their language study benefit from having this classification in their repertoire?

Discussion Notes

Chapter 7   Text Types

The third constraint that can be placed on searches is their text types. We can therefore search for words and constructions within a register, domain, genre, etc. As we will see, language choices are made, or made for us, by the social context in which a text comes into existence. In this chapter we explore linguistic features in a wide variety of corpora, each with own their textual metadata.

The texts that are included in corpora are the products of every speaker's or writer's idiolect. What shapes one's idiolect? Complete this diagram.

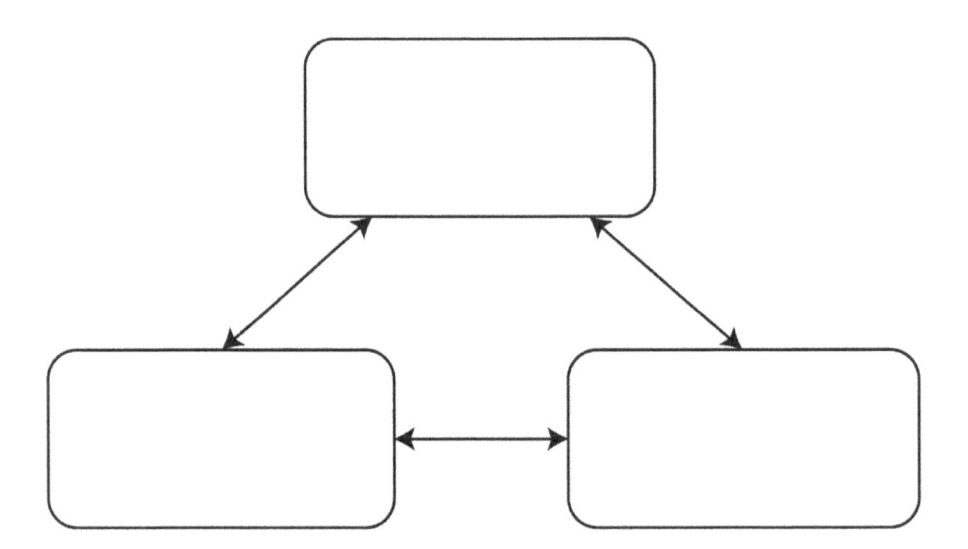

Questions from DESKE

Question 178   Can you answer any of the bullet point questions at the beginning of the chapter, or glean any other information about the context of situation of Corp ex.106?

Question 179 What things are *proven* and who *proves* them?

Question 180 What things does science claim to *prove*?

Question 181 Why does *prove* have so many adjective complements?

Question 182 When *prove* is used in the passive, what are the agents?

Question 183 Is there any difference in the use of *prove* in the domains of research and of maths?

Question 184 What differences can you identify in the uses of *prove* and the noun form, *proof*, in law compared with scientific research?

Question 185 How do sentences start in different genres?

Question 186 Are *moreover* and *whereas* used in speech or do they belong to the written language?

Question 187 In what domains does the collocation *clench teeth* most commonly occur?

Question 188 When are words spelled with hyphens?

Question 189 Who says or writes *to be well pleased*?

Question 190 Is it true that *above-mentioned* and *aforementioned* are used in written and spoken language respectively?

Question 191 How often does *see* mean *understand* and how often does it refer to sight?

Question 192 Which countries have the most TLDs in enTenTen?

Question 193   Which varieties of English use *the high street*?

Question 194   Can we identify sexist language through suffixes?

Question 195   Is *man* still used as a verb?

Question 196   When did English lose the final *e* in the spelling of many common words?

Question 197   When did *publish* enter the language?

Question 198   What are some words that have disappeared from English?

Question 199   Can this diachronic corpus enrich our understanding of *does not a*?

Question 200   Marriage equality for all?

Question 201   How do authors report the way things are *said* in fiction?

Question 202   Which adverbs express the purpose of saying, and which indicate the way something was said?

Question 203   Which verbs are followed by *that* in science writing?

Question 204   *Ubiquitous* looks like a rather specialised word. Is it?

Question 205   Is *data* used as a singular noun, plural or both?

Question 206   Is the phrase *having said that* mostly at the beginning of utterances?

Question 207   Did I really hear someone say *could of done* something?

Question 208   Did I really hear someone say *never heard nothing*?

Question 209   Both *at the weekend* and *on the weekend* are in the BNC but with quite different frequencies.

Question 210   Do men say *sorry* more than women?

Question 211   What are some common ways of starting sentences?

Question 212   Does the enTenTen corpus hold Australian texts?

Question 213   Is *battler* as Australian a word as many Australians think?

Quiz Questions: Language

Question 1:   **Which novel starts "It is a truth universally acknowledged ..."?**

   a. A Single Man (Isherwood)
   b. Too Much of a Good Thing (Roby)
   c. Pride and Prejudice (Austen)
   d. DESKE (Thomas)
   e. Hindsight (Karnes)

Question 2:   **Somebody proves something. Really?**

   a. this use of prove is quite rare
   b. this is the standard use of prove
   c. this construction is commonly used in science
   d. in law, detectives prove crimes

Question 3: Which varieties of English use *the high street*?

    a. UK
    b. Australia
    c. USA

Question 4: Marriage equality: are the collocates of *same-sex marriage* mostly ...

    a. vulgar
    b. antagonistic
    c. sociological
    d. legal
    e. religious

Question 5: Regional variation: Match these three words representing the same entity with their variety of English.

footpath	America
sidewalk	Britain
pavement	Australia

Question 6: What word is far more frequent at the beginning of utterances (spoken) than sentences (written)?

Quiz Questions: Linguistics

Question 1: What is meant by "primed idiolect"?

    a. language consists of hand-me-downs
    b. everyone's language is unique
    c. the way people use language is a result of their long-term exposure to language
    d. all of these options

Question 2: Which of the following statements are true of David Lee's Classification (DLC)?

    a. all corpora accessed through Sketch Engine use DLC
    b. David Lee created an algorithm that allows all corpora to be classified with his system
    c. DLC is more fine-grained than the BNC's own text classification

Question 3: Which part of speech most frequently follows *prove*?

    a. Noun
    b. Pronoun
    c. Verb
    d. Adjective

Question 4: Which of the following represent deixis?

    a. come and go
    b. here and there
    c. yesterday and tomorrow
    d. bring and take
    e. all of these

Question 5: Building the Brown Corpus was considered a waste of time and money, because ...

    a. computers were primitive in the 60s
    b. it was too small to yield any valuable findings
    c. it didn't contain any spoken language
    d. critics claimed that native speakers have enough intuition to answer questions
    e. corpus linguistics didn't exist at that time

Question 6: What is meant by sexist language?

    a. language used to seduce someone
    b. treating men and women as linguistic equals
    c. a result of feminism in the 1970s
    d. the verbal equivalent of Viagra
    e. language that uses male forms as the default for people in general

Research and Discussion Questions

A. What can you say about the Knobson corpus example (106) in terms of the bullet points at the beginning of Chapter 7?

B. If we accept O'Grady's statement, how would this impact on what and/or how we teach foreign languages?

O'Grady: Everyday language is not a collection of freely constructed novel sentences but is instead built up out of combinations of ready-made regularities previously experienced by the speaker and pre-existing in the discourse.

C. Can you envisage any use for diachronic corpus findings in foreign language teaching?

Discussion Notes

Chapter 8   Corpus Query Language in detail

This chapter aims to demystify the process of constructing powerful, multi-faceted queries. While they may look formidable at first sight, by this stage of DESKE it is not difficult to appreciate their structure, and consequently their potential. As with most chapters so far, these new resources open new doors to queries about other aspects of language and linguistics.

Questions from DESKE

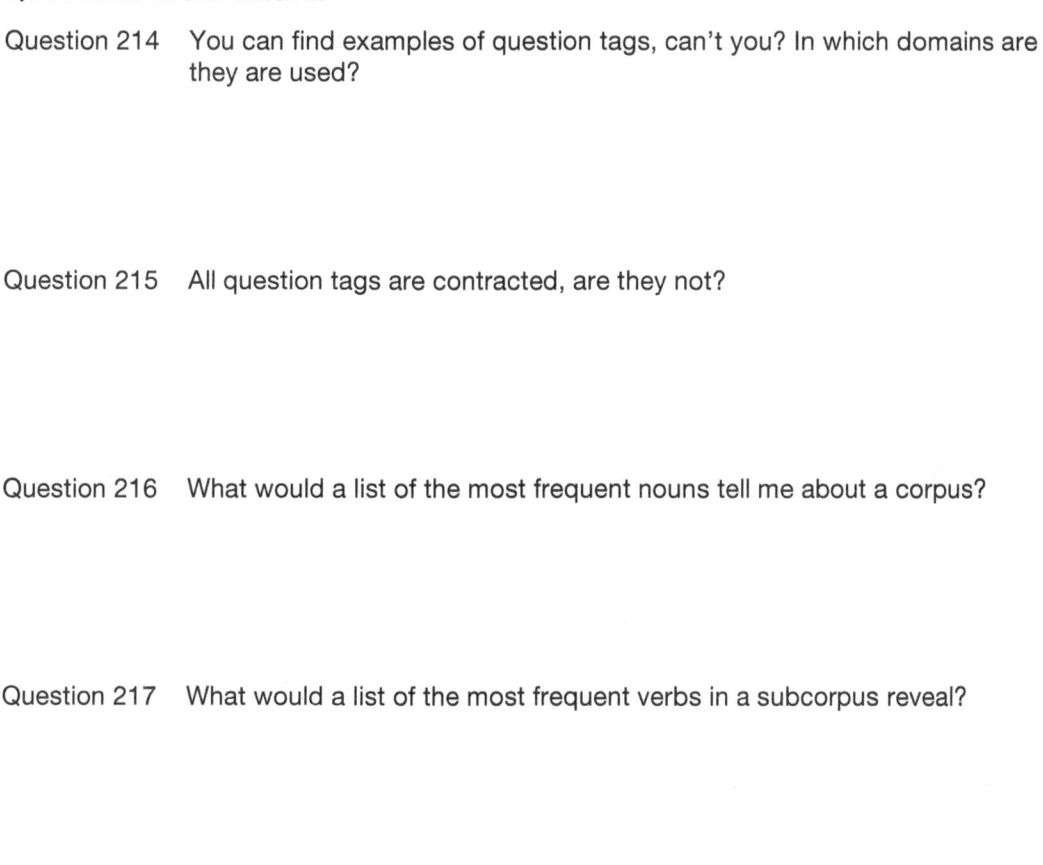

Question 214   You can find examples of question tags, can't you? In which domains are they are used?

Question 215   All question tags are contracted, are they not?

Question 216   What would a list of the most frequent nouns tell me about a corpus?

Question 217   What would a list of the most frequent verbs in a subcorpus reveal?

Question 218   What do we like | love | etc. doing?

Question 219   Are there any differences between adverbs that precede and follow verbs?

Question 220   Can I have a list of nouns ending in "f"?

Question 221   Did I just read the word *themself*?

Question 222   What prepositions follow *impact*?

Question 223   What prepositions follow these near synonyms?

Question 224   Is it the case that verbs following prepositions always use the –ing form?

Question 225   We noted earlier that *way how* was not a pattern of normal usage. What nouns do precede *way*?

Question 226   Is this curious structure, noun + preposition + and + noun + preposition, a pattern in English?

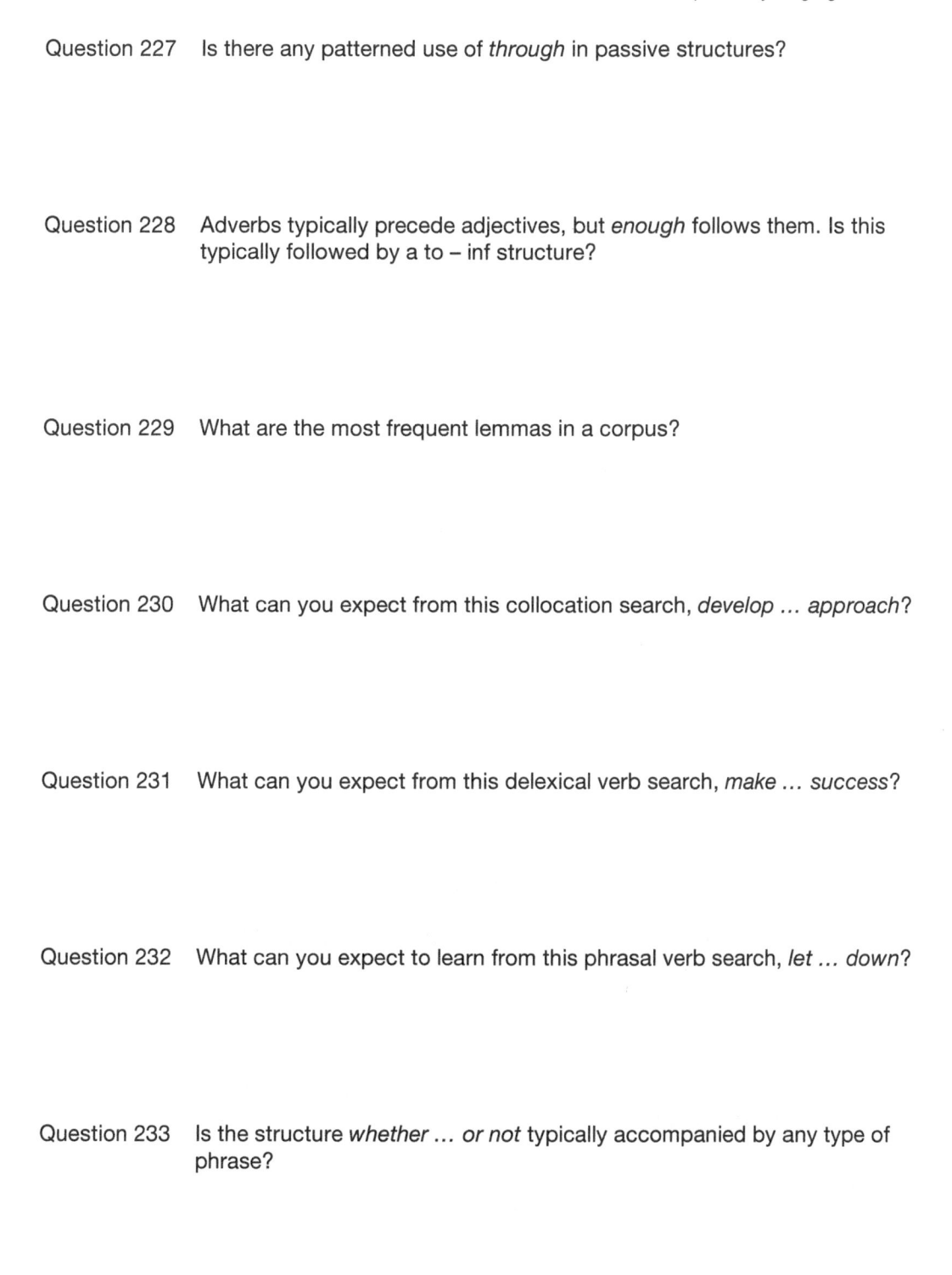

Question 227   Is there any patterned use of *through* in passive structures?

Question 228   Adverbs typically precede adjectives, but *enough* follows them. Is this typically followed by a to – inf structure?

Question 229   What are the most frequent lemmas in a corpus?

Question 230   What can you expect from this collocation search, *develop ... approach*?

Question 231   What can you expect from this delexical verb search, *make ... success*?

Question 232   What can you expect to learn from this phrasal verb search, *let ... down*?

Question 233   Is the structure *whether ... or not* typically accompanied by any type of phrase?

Question 234   Is the structure, as ___ a ___ as, frequent enough in the repertoire of native speakers to recognize it as a useful pattern?

Question 235   What parts of speech does *fast* function in apart from adjective?

Question 236   Is *which* always preceded by a comma?

Question 237   The split infinitive is wrong. Says who?

Question 238   Which adverbs do not end in –ly?

Question 239   What do the two spellings, *blond* and *blonde*, indicate?

Question 240   *Who* or *whom*?

Question 241   How much sense can be made of a string of proforms?

Question 242   When *only* is used at the beginning of a sentence, what follows?

Question 243   Do sentences in academic prose start with "I"?

Question 244   How are things said in fiction?

Question 245   How is the ampersand used in English?

Question 246   Which text types most typically have single words appearing between brackets?

Question 247   How far apart can whether ... or not be within a sentence?

Question 248   What are the most frequent parts of speech in a corpus?

Question 249 What are the most frequent syntagms?

Question 250 How do I find grammar structures like the present perfect or the third conditional in corpora?

Question 251 It is said that American English uses the present perfect less than British English.

Question 252 Are there any particular adverbs used with the present perfect progressive?

Question 253 Do any lexical patterns appear in the third conditional?

Question 254 Which words trigger the mandative subjunctive?

Question 255 Is it true that academic prose prefers the passive?

Question 256   Is the structure of the phrase, *drink someone beautiful*, a pattern of normal usage?

Question 257   Which verbs are used in ditransitive structures?

Question 258   Are there any patterns of normal usage associated with the order of verbs and their adverbs?

Question 259   What can we learn about IFIDs?

Quiz Questions: Language

Question 1:   **Adverbs ending in -ly tend to be ...**

   a. describing/modifying verbs
   b. describing/modifying adjectives
   c. more lexical than functional
   d. morphologically related to adjectives
   e. all of the options provided.

Question 2:   **Words ending in f ...**

   a. nouns change f to v when they decline
   b. verbs change f to v when they conjugate
   c. vowels change before the new ending is added
   d. some of the above is true sometimes
   e. none of the above is true sometimes

Question 3:   **Is *themself* used in both spoken and written language, in the BNC?**

   a. mostly spoken
   b. only spoken

Question 4: Verbs following prepositions always use the –ing form.

    a. True
    b. False

Question 5: Is the structure NOUN of NOUN relatively more frequent in ...

    a. informative texts
    b. imaginative texts

Question 6: What do the two spellings, blond and blonde, indicate?

    a. part of speech
    b. gender
    c. no difference

Quiz Questions: Linguistics

Question 1: Syntagms consist of ...

    a. parts of speech only
    b. parts of speech and lexical words
    c. parts of speech and function words
    d. lemmas and parts of speech

Question 2: Do question tags always contain contractions?

    a. mostly
    b. never
    c. always
    d. it depends on the speaker

Question 3: What does lempos mean?

    a. lemma + part of speech
    b. lemma + possessive

Question 4: Would you say that less frequent verbs of saying are semantically richer? (Q.244)

    a. Yes
    b. No

Question 5: Which of these points is not true of the mandative subjunctive?

    a. It is only used in written language
    b. It is more frequent in American than British English
    c. It is used after recommend, demand, important, proposal
    d. The verb form has no inflection in the so-called present
    e. It is used to express wishes, hypothesis, doubt, supposition

Research and Discussion Questions

A. What did you find out about adverbs that follow verbs? (Q.219)

B. What is serendipity? Can you think of any examples in your life in general, or your linguistic life?

C. Choose three phrasal verbs in which the verbs and the particles are all different. Allow between 0 and 3 tokens to occur between them. What do you observe about the separability of each of them?

D. Do you find that the semantics of the adverbs contribute to the semantics of the present perfect progressive?

E. Do any lexical patterns appear in the third conditional?

Discussion Notes

Chapter 9   Parallel Corpora

This relatively new feature of Sketch Engine is particularly valuable for comparing constructions in pairs of languages. Thanks to Sketch Engine's access to Opus2 parallel corpora, many languages can be compared with each other. Many of the questions asked earlier in the book from a purely monolingual English point of view, can be revisited with another language in mind. Questions at all levels of the Hierarchy of Language can be explored.

Questions from DESKE

Question 260   What might a parallel corpus contribute to our exploration of countability?

Question 261   How do the various meanings and uses of polysemous lexemes manifest in another language?

Question 262   Is there any consistency in the translation of grammar patterns?

Question 263   Do translated words have the same connotations and/or semantic prosody that they have in English?

Question 264   We have already explored some examples of litotes. Is this figure of speech peculiar to English?

Question 265   How have translators dealt with common words and phrases that do not have one-to-one translation equivalents?

Question 266   What are the applications of some common politeness expressions?

Question 267   How is the English future expressed when the source language has a future tense?

Question 268   How are the different meanings of *for the last time* expressed?

Question 269   How different are the meanings of *in the beginning* and *at the beginning*?

Question 270   How are English grammatical structures expressed in other languages?

Question 271   How do question tags manifest in translations in other languages?

Question 272   Do hypernyms extend across languages?

Question 273   Would transliterating a phrase into another language sound idiomatic?

Quiz Questions: Language & Linguistics

Question 1: What type of corpus has translated texts as well as the source language?

Question 2: English, Czech, German and Italian are the only languages available in the Opus suite?

a. True
b. False

Question 3: Is the Opus suite of corpora the only parallel ones available in SKE?

a. Yes
b. No

Question 4: Does *galore* have a positive or negative prosody? Search for its equivalents in other language and observe its prosody.

a. positive
b. negative
c. it depends on the language

Question 5: Hypernym-hyponym relationships are quite consistent across languages and relatively easy to translate.

a. True
b. False

Research and Discussion Questions

A. Can you suggest any approaches to using parallel corpora in language teaching? Do any caveats come to mind?

B. Comment on how the five given patterns of *manage* appear in another language that you know.

C. Revisit some of the lexical gaps you noted in earlier chapters and observe how translators have dealt with them.

Discussion Notes

Chapter 10 Collocation

Collocation is arguably the most pervasive linguistic construct in British linguistics in the last 100 years. The term is defined variously according to traditions and needs. DESKE has arrived at a rather prescriptive definition, referred to as the Two Lexeme Collocation (TLC), which precludes overlapping with multi-word units and colligation. The collocation tool in Sketch Engine, however, is not so constrained, rather it generates collocate lists of any node that can be constructed from the main query page. Once again, further aspects of language and linguistics can be explored through this new resource.

Questions from DESKE

Question 274   The Naked Gun! What else can be *naked* apart from people?

Question 275   What are the collocates of *open door policy*?

Question 276   How far apart can a node and its collocates be?

Question 277   Does *flying colours* refer to flags?

Question 278   What do the top T-score items tell us about the adjective *eligible*?

Question 279   Is inventing something normally considered a positive act?

Question 280   What do we think of Edward Snowden?

Question 281   Can you tell which meaning or use of your search word (node) is intended when it is paired with a collocate?

Question 282   How is the word *evidence* used differently in research and in law?

Question 283   When a word is polysemous, what activates its meanings in context?

Question 284   Does lexical support manifest across texts, or hover around certain words?

Question 285   What do the collocates of *bachelor* in its 'unmarried man' sense suggest about being one?

Quiz Questions: language

Question 1: Is *to spill ink* a ...

    a. collocation
    b. metaphor
    c. idiom
    d. colligation
    e. chunk

Question 2: What things do we *clench*?

    a. nose, toes and fingernails
    b. buttocks, fist and jaw
    c. books, plates and sofas
    d. lap, chest and stomach
    e. all of these

Question 3: In a list of collocates of *naked* in the BNC, which types of nouns are most common?

    (Count the words - do not add up the co-occurrence count).
    a. abstractions, e.g. *truth, hostility*
    b. parts of the body, e.g. *breast, torso*
    c. people, e.g. *corpse, child*
    d. things, e.g. *bulb, rock*

Question 4: Is *naked eye* a ...

    a. collocation
    b. metaphor
    c. idiom
    d. colligation
    e. chunk

Question 5: What do the -ly adverbs collocating with the verb *peer* tell us?

    a. people peer so as to gain group membership
    b. peering is not something you do for fun
    c. people peer if the printed page is not clear
    d. people peer if they want to be noticed

Quiz Questions: Linguistics

Question 1: Is a verb + preposition e.g. *decide between*, a collocation or a colligation?

    a. collocation
    b. colligation

Question 2: Are word association lists another way of deriving collocation lists?

  a. Yes
  b. No

Question 3: What is a lexeme?

  a. a multi-word unit
  b. a unit of meaning
  c. a single word expressing a single concept
  d. the same as a lemma

Question 4: How many words are in a two lexeme collocation?

  a. 1
  b. 2
  c. at least 2
  d. 4
  e. the same as in a chunk

Question 5: Which of the following are considered collocations, as espoused in DESKE?

  a. phrasal verbs
  b. delexical verbs
  c. prepositional verbs
  d. compound nouns
  e. none of these

Question 6: Are collocates useful when inferring the meaning of an unknown lexeme?

  a. quite useful
  b. they contribute nothing
  c. they disambiguate a lexeme unequivocally

Question 7: A collocation list sorted by T-score mostly has at the top ...

  a. rare lexemes
  b. function words
  c. words similar to word association lists

Question 8: Mutual Information listings contain words that are ...

  a. not in the corpus at all
  b. common in the set range of the node word
  c. rare in the corpus but common with the node word
  d. synonymous

Question 9: **LogDice collocation listings ...**

    a. do not depend on the size of the corpus
    b. take the grammatical relationship between the node and collocate into account
    c. contain significant lexical and function words
    d. all of these things

Question 10: **What is meant by co-selection? When producing language, ...**

    a. we select words that go together
    b. our choices are not random
    c. we combine prefabricated chunks
    d. one choice influences another choice
    e. all of these

Research and Discussion Questions

A. What are some collocating verbs and adjectives of a multi-word unit consisting of three nouns?

Using CQL, make a list of lexemes that consist of N N N. Choose two, each from different domains, and provide their top three frequent collocating verbs and adjectives as well as their top three significant collocating verbs and adjectives. Describe your research and results in prose.

B. What is the relationship between the prosody of *invent* and its collocates?

C. How and why might language teachers use the Hoey Procedure?

D. Following the example of *bat* under Polysemy, choose another such word and comment on how the collocates indicate the various meanings of the word. Is this a task that language learners could do?

Discussion Notes

Chapter 11 Word sketches

Word Sketches subscribe to a more conventional definition of collocation than the collocation tool in the previous chapter. Word Sketches are the ultimate tool in collocation listing because the dozens of collocates are sorted into columns showing their grammatical/syntactic relationship with the node. This facilitates not only statements to be made about lexical combinations, but syntactic ones as well. The tool was originally designed with lexicography in mind, but given the lexical focus in contemporary language education, they are an invaluable tool for teachers, students and anyone developing learning material.

Questions from DESKE

Question 286   What *alleviates symptoms*?

Question 287   How do sentences continue after intransitive verbs?

Question 288   How many things can you learn about *sympathetic* and about English in general from studying the word in this format?

Question 289   Does *nuanced* have a place in your world view?

Question 290   Which column gives the clearest positive associations of *wicked*?

Question 291   Do the most significant words that accompany *humdinger* reveal its meaning?

Question 292   Do the two words occur in the same order each time?

Question 293   Why do people use *student* and *pupil* in the same syntactic slot?

Question 294   Who or what is responsible for a *decline*?

Question 295   Is *is responsible for* the standard pattern of this adjective?

Question 296   Do *decline's* free prepositions launch adverbial phrases?

Question 297 How do we find a specific phrasal verb through word sketches?

Question 298 Are there other 'synonymous' verbs that can be used with the objects of *carry out*?

Question 299 Is there any correlation between the transitivity and separability of phrasal verbs?

Question 300 Are nouns more often subjects than objects?

Question 301 What things *indicate* in academic prose?

Question 302 The phrasal verb, *blow up*, is quite polysemous – what things blow up?

Question 303 Who or what *analyses*?

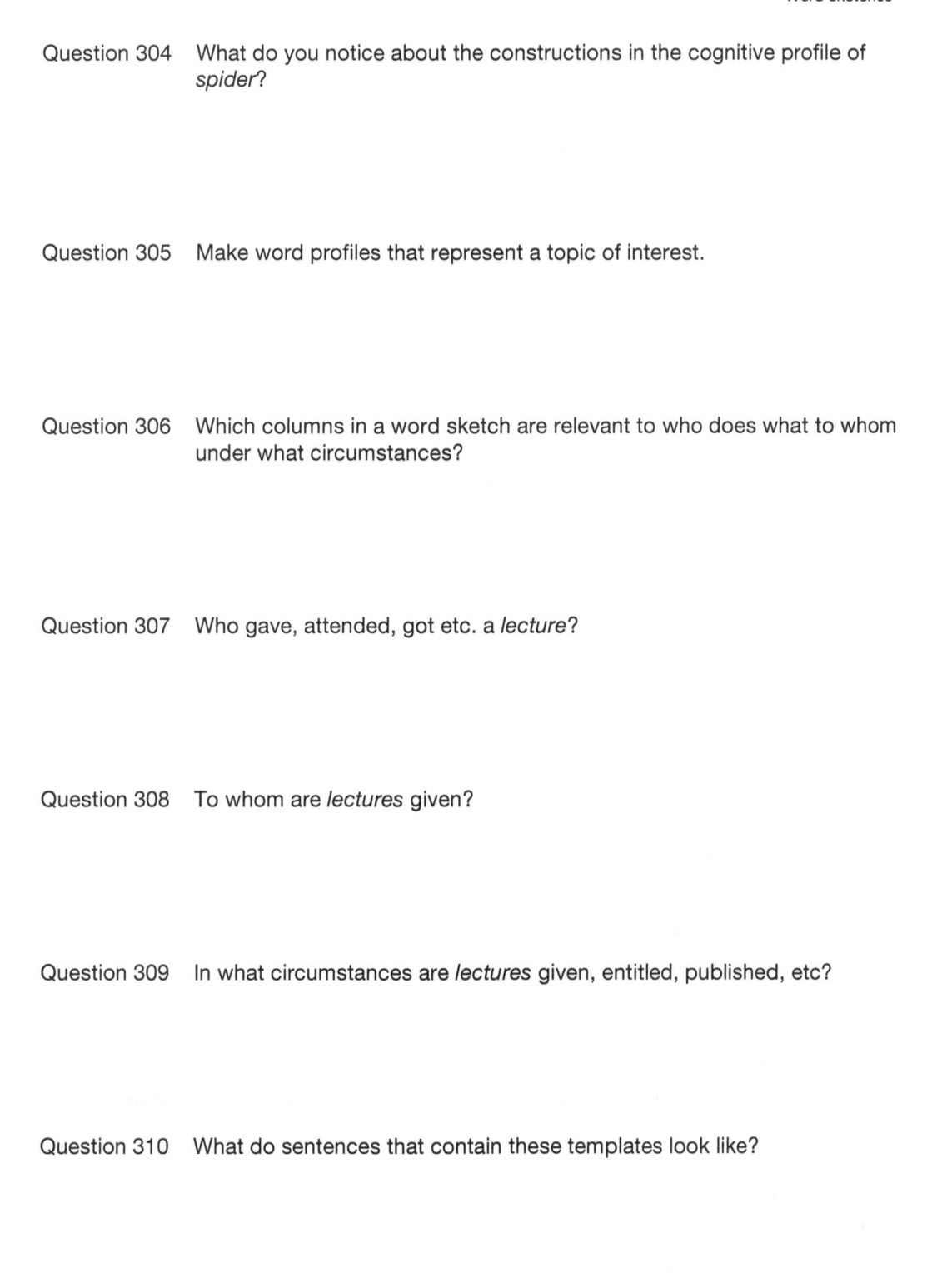

Question 304   What do you notice about the constructions in the cognitive profile of *spider*?

Question 305   Make word profiles that represent a topic of interest.

Question 306   Which columns in a word sketch are relevant to who does what to whom under what circumstances?

Question 307   Who gave, attended, got etc. a *lecture*?

Question 308   To whom are *lectures* given?

Question 309   In what circumstances are *lectures* given, entitled, published, etc?

Question 310   What do sentences that contain these templates look like?

Question 311 How do the text types in which *get a lecture* occurs support its non-academic tendencies?

Question 312 Is distinguishing the objects of verbs enough to disambiguate them?

Quiz Questions: Language

Question 1: What are the objects of *allay*?

a. symptoms
b. fear
c. transport
d. a welcome

Question 2: Multi-word sketches take us from collocation to 'collocations of collocations'.

Make a word sketch of *time*, then click on the bold word *waste*. Then in the multi-word sketch, click on the frequency of *money*. What preposition is most frequent after the chunk that emerges? And what follows that preposition?

a. waste time and money for
b. waste time and money by
c. waste time and money in
d. waste time and money on

Question 3: What things are people *responsible for*?

a. mainly abstract nouns
b. mainly concrete nouns
c. mainly people
d. mainly gerunds

Question 4: Which of these do not follow the intransitive phrasal verb *stand around*?

a. object
b. -ing forms
c. prepositional phrases of manner
d. prepositional phrases of place
e. punctuation

Question 5: **Is the phrasal verb *stand around* separable?**

   a. Yes
   b. No

Quiz Questions: Linguistics

Question 1: **Which of the following options in word sketches can make them learner friendly?**

   a. less data
   b. frequency sorting
   c. selecting specific gramrels
   d. all of the options provided.

Question 2: **Which part of speech carries most of the meaning of a text, is the most frequent in a text and in the language at large, as well as being the most open to new coinages?**

Question 3: **What role does English word order play in determining grammatical relationships?**

   a. subjects are noun phrases that have their own internal structure and precede the verb phrase
   b. objects are noun phrases that have their own internal structure and follow the verb phrase
   c. in passive structures the object assumes subject position
   d. prepositional phrases have their own internal structure and act as adverbials
   e. all of the options provided.

Question 4: **The words which are semantically richer in a word sketch are at the top of the lists when they are sorted by ...**

   a. score
   b. frequency

Question 5: **What is the result of clustering a word sketch?**

   a. words of the same part of speech are grouped
   b. words with similar frequencies are grouped
   c. words which are semantically related are grouped
   d. more words are added to the word sketch

Question 6: How much more frequent is *symptom* as a plural noun than as a singular noun?

a. twice as frequent
b. six times as frequent
c. ten times as frequent
d. it isn't

Question 7: How do word sketches indicate the grammatical relationships between the node and its collocates?

a. by showing each collocate with its part of speech
b. by providing a word template of each combination
c. by grouping the collocates according to the relationship
d. by sorting them by their part of speech

Question 8: Are predicative adjective structures only used with copular verbs?

a. Yes
b. No

Question 9: When used in discourse, which type of adjective provides new information about its noun?

a. attributive
b. predicative

Question 10: Why is the and/or relationship worth observing?

a. it is salient
b. it is a type of collocation
c. it instantiates native speaker usage
d. it is not random
e. all of the options provided.

Question 11: Which parts of speech have bound prepositions?

a. verbs
b. verbs and nouns
c. verbs and nouns and adjectives
d. verbs and nouns and adjectives and adverbs
e. all parts of speech

Question 12: What information about a word does its word template contain?

a. collocation
b. colligation
c. semantic types
d. word order
e. all of the options provided.

Question 13: In cognitive profiles, the collocates can be ...

    a. verbs
    b. adjective
    c. verbs and adjectives
    d. any part of speech
    e. verbs and adjectives and nouns

Question 14: What does a word template not express?

    a. modality
    b. deixis
    c. aspect
    d. mood
    e. all of the options provided.

Question 15: Which parts of speech can have word templates?

    a. nouns
    b. verbs
    c. adjectives
    d. all of the options provided.

Research and Discussion Questions

A. Create word templates of the verbs *miss* and *lack*. The aim is to help learners understand the differences in their meaning and usage.

B. Do word sketches indicate the transitivity of verbs? If so, how? And who wants to know?

C. Choose a noun that you teach to B2 students and prepare a list of questions similar to Q.288 that you could use with learners. What would they do with the answers? What would they learn in the process?

D. How can word sketch data be employed in the teaching of prepositions? Give some thought to what needs to be known about prepositions in order to teach/learn them effectively.

E. What use is clustering? What observations can be made?

F. Choose a noun that you might teach to B2 students. Using data from its word sketch, make a cognitive profile with up to ten sentences.

Discussion Notes

Chapter 12 Word sketch differences

Taking the idea of word sketches one step further, word sketch differences offers a search interface in which a pair of words can be entered to show on one page the similarities and differences in their collocations and colligation patterns. In fact, one further step permits comparing words in different registers.

Questions from DESKE

Question 313   What is the difference between *be interested* and *be interesting*?

Question 314   Should I describe something as *random* or *arbitrary*?

Question 315   How differently are *sexy* and *sexual* used?

Question 316   What are the similarities and differences between the uses of *convincing* and *persuasive*?

Question 317   What does English do with *co-operate* and *collaborate*?

Question 318   How do singular and plural forms differ in their usage?

Question 319   How is *discover* used in fiction and science?

Quiz Questions: Language & Linguistics

Question 1:   **Which gramrels have no content for *interested* in Sketch Diffs in the BNC?**

a. followed by the preposition *in*
b. followed by the preposition *to*
c. the and/or relationship
d. followed by the infinitive particle *to*

Question 2:   **In the *interested/interesting* Sketch Diffs in the BNC, there is one column that has plenty of red and green but no white collocates.**

a. adverbs
b. attributive adjectives
c. infinitives
d. adjectival complements
e. compound nouns

Question 3:   **Do *hand* and *hands* occur in the BNC in similar numbers?**

a. Yes
b. No

Question 4:   **Judging by the colours in the *hand/hands* Sketch Diff, are the two word forms used ...**

a. in the same lexical and grammatical contexts
b. quite similarly
c. quite differently

Question 5:   **The Sketch-Diff of *student* and *pupil* contains many "white words". What does this indicate?**

a. the two nouns occur with similar frequency in the corpus
b. they are semantically similar enough to have many collocates in common
c. that speakers do not distinguish between them

Research and Discussion Question

The Sketch diff of *interested/interesting* is a gold mine of data about this word. How might you use some of it to teach this often confused/confusing pair of adjectives to B2 students?

Chapter 13 Word list

Word list is a departure from the tools explored up to this point, inasmuch as this tool provides data about the corpus as a whole. It generates frequency lists of words, lemmas, part of speech tags, and anything else that is in the metadata of a given corpus. For example, the gender or age of a speaker, the authors of texts, nationality, where the texts were collected – whatever the metadata.

Word list is not particularly user-friendly as it has a lot features, which may appear unstable because the metadata in each corpus is different, and because the tools operates on several levels at once. It is a powerful tool if you are its master, not the other way around. Be patient!

Questions from DESKE

Question 320   Can I have a list of all the words in a corpus?

Question 321   Can I have a list of all the collocations in a corpus?

Question 322   What strings of words most frequently occur in the corpus?

Question 323   Are the most frequent words in written English more or less the same as in spoken English?

Question 324   What are the most frequent tags in the corpus?

Question 325   Do n-grams represent or instantiate the tenors, fields and modes of corpora?

Question 326   What are the most frequent syntagms in the corpus?

Question 327   How balanced are the attributes in the corpus?

Question 328   What noun tags are in the corpus and in what numbers?

Question 329   Which lemmas occur at least 2,000 times?

Question 330   Which words starting with *mega* are in the corpus once only?

Question 331   How many hapax legomena are there in a corpus?

Question 332   How many of the documents in the BNC are emails?

Question 333   What are the features of a particular set of words?

Question 334   Are words with the feminine suffix, -ess, fading from use?

Question 335   Which words in a corpus occur with a frequency similar to a given word?

Question 336   What nouns are in a corpus?

Question 337   Which words in a corpus are most 'key'?

Question 338   What are the key words in the Australian subcorpus?

Question 339   Which verbs occur not more than 2,000 times?

Question 340   Which adjectives occur between 1,450 and 1,550 times?

Question 341   How new and how frequent is the question tag, *innit*?

Quiz Questions: Language & Linguistics

Question 1: Match these corpora with the part of speech tag that is most frequent in them.

NN   LEC
PP   CHILDES
SENT   BNC Written subcorpus

Question 2: An n-gram of words creates ...

a. lexical bundles
b. syntagms
c. collocations
d. chunks

Question 3: How many of the documents in the BNC are emails?

a. 7
b. 70
c. 770
d. 7,000
e. 0

Question 4: Which nouns occur approximately 1,000 times as lemmas in the London English Corpus?

a. court, analysis, product, individual
b. person, course, job, football
c. understanding, machine, Sunday, organization

Research and Discussion Questions

A. Using the subcorpora in the English CHILDES corpus, what can you observe about the 4-grams used by 4 to 6 year olds compared with those used by 13 to 17 year olds? Also note if a caregiver is speaking.

B. Why do think that so many of the most frequent 4-word bundles in the BNC's fiction subcorpus contain *n't*?

C. In what situations might language teachers use some of the word lists functions?

Discussion Notes

Chapter 14 DIY corpora

This chapter takes readers step by step through the process of creating their own corpora from the internet at first, which involves providing key words, from which the WebBootCat software crawls the web collecting documents that are likely to be relevant to the topic. Alternatively, users may provide sets of URLs themselves.

The second method of building a corpus involves users uploading their own documents.

There are no questions for this chapter.

Chapter 15 Pride and Prejudice

This chapter users a corpus created by following steps in the previous chapter. A variety of questions is posed to develop a range of question types based on the language, linguistic and technical knowledge accumulated in the process of working through this book.

Questions from DESKE

Question 342   Does studying the language of classic literature cause learners to use words, phrase and structures in non-standard ways?

Question 343   What key words emerge when the novel is compared with enTenTen?

Question 344   What grammar, vocabulary and discourse features emerge from the novel's n-grams?

Question 345   Does Austen use *handsome* to describe men and women, and non-living things?

Question 346   What does *amends* mean?

Question 347   Do question tags feature in the dialogue?

Question 348   To what use are modal verbs put in this novel?

Question 349   Is shall used exclusively with first person pronouns?

Question 350   What features of reported speech can be observed in this novel?

Question 351   What positive adjectives does Austen use to describe people?

Question 352   Are the D'Arcys ever referred to with their first names?

Question 353   Does Austen typify her characters by what she has them do?

Question 354   Are some characters more prone to not making answers than others?

Glossary

Term Warfare

In many fields, and linguistics is no exception, we often come across the same phenomena with a variety of terms. For example, linguists say that English has two tenses in contrast to language educators who conflate **tense** and **aspect** (progressive and perfect) and sometimes **voice** (active and passive) to arrive at a much higher number of 'tenses'. The terms **conversion, zero derivation** and **zero-affixation** all refer to the use of the same word form in different parts of speech, as we see in fast in the following: *a fast car, to run fast, be on a fast, to fast.* In terms of discourse, the same word or phrase may be referred to as **conjuncts** and **discourse markers**, **signposting**, **Organisation/Orientation language**. In lexical studies, terms for multi-word units such as **multi-word unit, lexeme, chunk, phrase, bundle** are often used interchangeably or their definitions them overlap. We also have **colligation, grammar pattern, template, collostructions**, all of which involve collocation and colligation and despite not being interchangeable, have fairly fuzzy borders. Fuzzy borders or 'grey areas' between concepts is the extent to which the semantic field of one **word/term/lexeme** trespasses on that of another.

The language feature that we search for in corpora is referred to as the **search word** or **search item** or **node**, whereas in standard concordance pages it is referred to as the **key word**, a term that has quite a different meaning in text studies. And research in lexical semantics attempts to describe the systematic influences that words have on each others' meanings and uses the terms **semantic prosody, semantic preference** and **attitudinal preference**.

It is not surprising that people who work closely with concepts, as scientists do, find that existing terminology does not express the nuances that our work demands. Hence, new terms and new uses of old terms.

Sources

In addition to the author's own definitions and Wikipedia, the following sources have been consulted in constructing this glossary.

Crystal, D. (2008). A Dictionary of Linguistics and Phonetics (6th ed.). Oxford: Wiley-Blackwell.

McEnery, T., & Hardie, A. (2012). Corpus linguistics: method, theory and practice. Cambridge: Cambridge University Press.

McEnery, T., Xiao, R., & Tono, Y. (2006). Corpus-based language studies: An advanced resource book. London: Routledge.

Saeed, J. I. (2016). Semantics (4th ed.). Oxford: Wiley-Blackwell.

Yule, G. (2014). The Study of Language (5th ed.). Cambridge: Cambridge University Press.

adjective: a type of word identifying an attribute of a noun. When in the noun phrase, it is an attributive adjective, when used after a copular verb, it is a predicative adjective providing new information.

adjunct: a noun phrase or preposition phrase which adds additional information about the state-of-affairs in a clause, without being one of the arguments (or participants) of the verb.

adverb: a word which characteristically modifies a verb to indicate how, where, when, etc. the verb is performed, or an adjective to indicate degree. Adverb is also used as a hold-all for other words such as *ago, not, so, twice*. Sentence adverbs are words that express the speaker's attitude/orientation, e.g. *undoubtedly*, and signposting/organisation e.g. *firstly*.

adverbial: an element of syntax that is not usually part of the clause. It expresses the circumstance of a clause, e.g. how, where, when, and the discourse organisation and pragmatic orientation language.

affix: superordinate for prefix and suffix.

affordance: each learning opportunity that a text offers is an affordance. For example, a text can be exploited to study all four skills and four systems.

anaphor: a pronoun or noun which refers to an entity that it does not specifically name, something that has already been mentioned in the preceding discourse. See also cataphora.

argument: a noun phrase or preposition phrase which indicates one of the participants in the state-of-affairs of the clause. This includes the subject, object, indirect object and so on. In traditional grammar, the argument noun phrases are often said to be compulsory elements of the clause syntax.

article: a word that specifies whether a noun is definite or indefinite.

aspect: a semantic system that allows different viewpoints on the time of an event or situation, e.g. perfective, continuous.

attributive adjective: an adjective that modifies a noun within a noun phrase (see predicative adjective).

attested language: language that was produced in a genuine communicative situation as opposed to language invented for the purpose of illustration.

auxiliary verb: a category of grammatical words; they do not indicate any particular 'action' but instead mark features of the tense, aspect or modality of a main verb

balance: a corpus is said to be balanced if the relative sizes of each of its subsections have been chosen with the aim of adequately representing the range of language that exists in the population of texts being sampled.

base form: the base form of a word does not have any inflections (e.g. –s, -d) or **affix**es (e.g. dis-, il- -ship, -esque). This is the form of a word that corresponds to dictionary entries. In corpus studies, it corresponds to **lemma**.

binomial: consists of two words from the same grammatical category coordinated by *and* or *or*, and that occur frequently as a unit, e.g. *wear and tear*. A **trinomial** consists of three such elements, e.g. *healthy, wealthy and wise*.

breadcrumb trail: a navigation tool in a browser that allows a user to see where the current page is in relation to the website's hierarchy. Used extensively in Sketch Engine.

bundle: lexical bundles are strings of word forms that commonly occur together in natural discourse. They do not aim to represent a complete structural or pragmatic unit and they often extend across structural units.

cataphora: a cross-referring noun or pronoun that refers to an entity that is introduced subsequently in the discourse.

chunk: a group of words that is complete as a semantic, discourse or pragmatic unit. It words do not require morphological changes and in most cases do not even permit change. It is stored in memory as a single holistic unit.

cognate: a language or linguistic form that is historically derived from the same source as another, e.g. Spanish and French are 'cognate languages', both deriving from Latin.

colligation: the colligation of a particular word is its relationship with grammatical markers and grammatical categories. Grammatical company includes such things as a bound preposition, a wh- or that clause, infinitive, -ing forms, use in passive. For example, *deter from; be familiar with, motivate s.o. + inf.. protect* + reflexive pronoun. These are syntagmatic features of language.

collostruction: a co-occurrence relationship between a grammatical construction (the collostruct) and a lemma that tends to occur in one of its slots (the collexeme).

collocation: this paradigmatic feature of language is defined variously. Most definitions of collocation include, "a pair of words that frequently co-occur" and limit the 'words' in collocations to lexical words (noun, verbs, adjectives, adverbs), including multi-word lexemes. DESKE refers to this as the "two lexeme collocation" (TLC).

collocation plus: this takes the TLC definition (two lexeme collocation) of **collocation** as the starting point for syntax: when the pair of **lexeme**s is a noun and a verb, in either order, this is regareded as the kernel of a clause.

comparability: two corpora or subcorpora are said to be comparable if their sampling frames are similar or identical. For example, a corpus of 1 million words of English news text and a corpus of 1 million words of French news text are comparable for the purpose of contrasting English and French.

componential analysis: the analysis of vocabulary into a finite set of basic elements or components.

computational linguistics: the field of research applying computer science techniques to language and language data. This includes, but is not limited to, various kinds of research using corpora, such as text mining. (Despite the name, computational linguistics is very often in practice a branch of computer science rather than a branch of linguistics.)

concordance: a display of every instance of a specified word or other search item found in a corpus, together with a given amount of preceding and following context for each result or 'hit'.

concordancer: a computer program that produces a concordance from a specified text or corpus. Most concordance software can also facilitate more advanced analyses.

connotation: in addition to the basic, objective meaning of a word, many words carry additional subjective ideas or emotions. This is a property of a word that is typically shared across the language-user community.

construction: see construction grammar

construction grammar: a theory of grammar within cognitive linguistics, where all syntactic structures and idioms are considered to be constructions – meaningful units, stored in the mental lexicon, which may consist of concrete words as well as abstract slots; in this view language is produced by combining together words and constructions, linking them via the slots in the constructions.

contraction: a shortened linguistic element attached to an adjacent form and indicated by an apostrophe, e.g. *can't, would've.*

corpus: (plural corpora), a corpus is a collection of language representative of a particular variety of language or genre which is sampled and stored in electronic form for analysis using concordance software.

corpus-based: where corpora are used to test preformed hypotheses or exemplify existing linguistic theories. It can refer to either: (a) any approach to language that uses corpus data and methods, or (b) an approach to linguistics that uses corpus methods but does not subscribe to corpus-driven principles.

corpus-driven: an inductive process where corpora are investigated from the bottom up and patterns found therein are used to explain linguistic regularities and exceptions of the language variety/genre exemplified by those corpora.

co-text: the words and structures that accompany the node, which can be observed by studying concordance pages vertically. Co-text is a paradigmatic aspect of a word's usage.

context: refers to the text to the left and right of the node when we read the extracts horizontally. Studying language as a linear sequence is referred to as syntagmatic analysis. See **syntagm**.

conversion: a standard property of English word forms is that they function as more than one part of speech. For example, many –ing forms of verbs are used as adjectives and nouns. It also referred to as functional shift and zero derivation. From a corpus perspective, conversion complicates POS tagging.

core English: the body of English that is common to all varieties, including features of syntax and lexis, standard idioms, phonology, discourse markers and cultural references.

countability: count nouns usually refer to items, can be individuated, used with the indefinite article, and made plural. Non-count nouns cannot and often refer to substances and abstractions. Nouns can be both count and non-count in different contexts.

data-driven learning: a way of using corpora in language teaching that involves the learners being given direct access to corpora and a tool for searching them, the intention being that their exploration of the corpus enriches their language learning and learner autonomy.

David Lee's classification: indicates genres, registers, text types, domains and styles. It superseded the BNC's classification of text types.

declension: a set of nouns, adjectives or pro-nouns that share the same base form when declined.

deixis: features of language that refer directly to the personal, temporal, or locational characteristics of the situation, their deictic forms, e.g. *you, now, here.*

delexical verb: a structure also known as light verb. It consists of a verb and a noun phrase in which the meaning is carried by the noun, e.g. *give a smile, have a bath, take a photo.*

diachronic: relating to the study of a language or languages as they change over time. A diachronic corpus samples texts across a span of time or from multiple time periods. See also **synchronic**.

discourse: in the most basic sense, a discourse is a stretch of language longer than a single sentence. By extension, the term has a range of other meanings: an entire text; the whole of a population of texts; or a way of using language or way of thinking about the world. It is also defined as an instance of spoken or written language that has describable internal relationships of form and meaning that relate coherently to an external communicative function or purpose and a given audience/interlocutor.

discourse marker: a word or phrase that is used to organise a text and/or orientate the reader. For example, *furthermore, and what's more, as you may have heard, which in turn, contrary to popular belief, surprisingly, and finally.*

dysfluency: an irregularity in spoken language production that typically produces a sentence that, according to traditional grammar, would not be considered well-formed. Dysfluencies include false starts, utterances broken off halfway or reformulated halfway through, slips of the tongue, fillers such as um and er, and other phenomena arising from the unplanned, spontaneous nature of spoken language.

ditransitive: the ditransitive is a grammatical structure where a verb is linked to two objects, the direct object and the indirect object, as well as a subject. This ditransitive construction, of the form (someone) [verb] (someone) (something), alternates with the for-dative construction (someone) (verb) (something) to (someone). A ditransitive verb is one that occurs in these two structures, for example *give* or *send*.

disjunct: a sentence adverbial that conveys e speaker's attitude to the content of what they are saying.

domain: the situation in which language is used. e.g. family domain, work domain.

encoding: the process of representing the structure of a text using markup language and annotation.

emergentist: a view of language acquisition where grammar emerges from experience of language via general learning processes, rather than being an innate function of the mind or a mental module that is independent of general cognition.

factotum: is a category of words that do not belong to a specific domain, but rather they can appear in almost all of them. See **general noun.**

FASI: when learning a foreign language, steps are always being taken towards becoming: Fluent, Accurate, Sophisticated, Idiomatic.

fluency: smooth, rapid, effortless use of language.

frequency list: a list of all the items that are returned from a corpus search together with a count of how often each occurs.

functionalism: an approach to linguistic theory which seeks to explain the forms of language structures by reference to how they are used, involving such factors as communicative purposes, how utterances are processed and so on.

general noun: the class of general noun is a small set of nouns having generalized reference within the major noun classes, those such as human noun, place noun, fact noun.

generative grammar: any theory of grammar which aims to define a set of formal rules that can generate all and only the grammatical sentences of a given language or of all languages. These theories of grammar are inspired ultimately by the work of Noam Chomsky.

genre: see register.

given information: words in a sentence that refer to entities or events that have already been introduced into the discourse and can be assumed to be in the speaker's and hearer's minds, express given information.

glue: pre-processing of corpora involves separating punctuation from the words they are attached to. Sketch Engine offers the structure <g> (glue) which can be selected so as to remove the resulting gaps from concordance pages.

grammar pattern: the characteristic grammatical company that words keeps. At the level of a single word, this is colligation; groups of semantically related words tend to keep the same company and form patterns.

grammatization: when we want to express ourselves, key words appear in our minds. In order to turn these few words into a comprehensible Message, we have to grammatize the words. This involves selecting collocating words, and colligating structures to generate the words' templates. It further involves selecting tense and aspect, determiners and deictic elements that situate the Message in its context.

grammaticalisation: the process whereby, typically over a period of centuries, content words can lose their main meaning and become grammatical elements, usually accompanied by phonetic reduction. In English, for example, all auxiliary verbs that mark aspect or modality in the modern language are derived from what were once lexical verbs that could stand alone as the main verb of the clause.

gramrel: short for grammatical relationship. This is used in Sketch Engine's logdice statistics and word sketches.

guided discovery: a teaching procedure in which teachers provide learners with the tools and sources to discover the answers to pre-set questions. See Kibbitzer.

head: in the syntactic analysis of phrases, one word is usually identified as the head or main word. The grammatical properties of this word determine the grammatical properties of the phrase, for example, an adjective phrase behaves grammatically much like a lone adjective, a noun phrase like a lone noun.

headword: see lemma and base-form.

Hoey procedure: this is a verification procedure. It uses corpus data to determine how entrenched chunks that appear in a text are in the language at large. In Hoey's *Lexical Priming* (2005), he demonstrates why one wording of a sentence sounds more natural or idiomatic than another. The term Hoey Procedure was created by the author of DESKE, with the professor's permission.

hypertext: text containing links that can be followed to navigate around a document or between documents. The World Wide Web is essentially a massive collection of hypertext.

idiolect: the linguistic system of an individual speaker.

idiom: a phrase or other multi-word unit whose meaning cannot be deduced simply by combining the meanings of the words within it; most theories of language agree that for this reason, idioms and their meanings must be part of the lexicon of the language.

Idiom principle: the idea in neo-Firthian linguistics that most language is produced and comprehended by linear chaining-together of idiomatic elements drawn from the lexicon. In this view, much less language is produced or comprehended by building clauses around words according to abstract rules of grammar. This latter procedure is known as the Open-choice Principle.

illustrative sentences: a sentence used to illustrate the meaning and usage of a word or structure. Corpora provide many attested sentences that have pragmatic and discourse veracity that invented ones do not.

intransitive: a verb that does not take a direct object. The intransitive construction is the grammatical structure, found in many languages, of a clause containing a verb and its subject but no objects. Verbs of motion are a salient group.

introspection: this involves making intuitive judgements about whether a given sentence is grammatical.

keyword: a word that occurs more frequently in a text than in the language generally. A reference corpus is used to determine this statistically.

key word in context (KWIC): a way of displaying a node word or search term in relation to its context within a text or corpus. This usually means the node is displayed centrally in a table with co-text displayed in columns to its left and right. Here, 'key word' means 'search term' and is distinguished from keyword.

kibbitzer: a teaching procedure developed by Tim Johns, in which he investigated language problems in a student's writing by searching for particular lexical items or phrases in a suitable corpus. See also Hoey Procedure.

Ll: first language, native language, mother tongue.

L2: second language, a language learnt after early childhood.

learner corpus (LC): a corpus containing texts of language produced by language learners. Such corpora are used for second language acquisition research and its applications.

lemma: a group of word forms that are related by being inflectional forms of the same base word. The lemma is usually referred to by base or stem. e.g. *destroy, destroys, destroying* and *destroyed* are all part of the verb lemma *destroy*, but the noun *destruction* is a separate lemma, because it is related to *destroy* by derivational rather than inflectional processes. The notion of a headword, as found in a dictionary, is generally equivalent to that of a lemma. See also word family.

lemmatisation: a form of corpus annotation where every token in a corpus is labelled to indicate its lemma.

lexeme: a unit of meaning whether expressed by a single word e.g. *fruit*, or a multi-word unit, e.g. *the day before yesterday*. Lexemes cannot be equated with words.

lempos: term created by splicing **lemma** and **POS**, the acronym for part of speech. Lempos is one of the formats that the Sketch Engine offers in various droplists, along with word, lemma, etc. Lempos lists contain the lemma and a one-letter POS indicator, e.g. destroy-v.

lexical bundles: a type of n-gram containing word forms only.

lexical item: either (a) a general term for a lemma or anything else found in the mental lexicon, or (b) in neo-Firthian theory, another term for the extended unit of meaning.

lexical set: used in language pedagogy for groups of words and phrases that belong to a particular topic, e.g. travel, hair styles, sport.

lexical support: when words with similar connotations are used in the same context, they support each other and strengthen its illocutionary force.

lexicogrammar: a term used in systemic functional linguistics (SFL) to emphasize the interdependence of, and continuity between, vocabulary (lexis) and syntax (grammar) and including morphology.

lexis: the words and other meaningful units, such as idioms, in a language. The lexis or vocabulary of a language in usually viewed as being stored in a kind of mental dictionary, the lexicon.

linear unit grammar: LUG divides stretches of language into (a) Messages and (b) units of Organisation/Orientation. The Message units are subdivided into various types of fragments which pertain especially to the incremental co-construction of messages in speech. However, this linear, non-hierarchical approach applies equally to written and spoken language.

logDice: a collocation statistic used in Sketch Engine, it observes the grammatical relationship between the node and the collocate, and is not affected by the size of the corpus.

machine-readable text: text represented as sequences of characters encoded as numbers in computer memory or saved in a disk file. Image files are not machine-readable in this sense.

manual annotation: the method of corpus annotation where the analytic codes are added to the text by a human being.

marked/unmarked: linguistic constructions exist in binary oppositions. The more basic of the two is usually more frequent and less surprising – this is the unmarked choice a speaker may make. A marked alternation conveys more layers of meaning by deviating from the norm and is therefore more salient.

markup codes: inserted into a corpus file to indicate features of the original text other than the actual words of the text. In a written text, for example, markup might include paragraph breaks, omitted pictures, and other aspects of layout.

meaning potential: out of context, a word has a number of meanings, its meaning potential, which is disambiguated or realised in context. Context may be the situation, collocation, colligation, etc.

metadata: data about the texts that are in a corpus, which typically include title, author, date of publication, and may also include information about the sex, age and social class of speakers, the internet domains from which texts were downloaded.

metacognitive strategies: these are methods used to help students think about their thinking and understand the way they learn.

metalanguage: the language used for describing or analysing a language, thus linguistic terminology.

modal verb: an auxiliary verb which marks some feature of modality on another, main verb. Different types of modality indicate permission, obligation, possibility, ability, necessity and other notions of this type. In addition to the central modal verbs, e.g. *may, must, can*, there are others such as *dare, have to, had better, be supposed to, used to.*

monitor corpus: a corpus that grows continually, with new texts being added over time so that the dataset continues to represent the most recent state of the language as well as earlier periods.

morpheme: the smallest contrastive unit of grammar, e.g. man, de-, -tion, -s, etc.

mutual information: a statistic that indicates how strong the link between two things is. Mutual information can be used to calculate collocations by indicating the strength of the co-occurrence relationship between a node and collocate.

neo-Firthian: a label for the tradition of corpus linguistics based on the work on John Sinclair, who applied the ideas of J. R. Firth to corpus analysis. Two central ideas in the approach to corpus linguistics favoured by neo-Firthian linguists are collocation and discourse.

new information. words in a sentence that introduce entities or events that have not previously been mentioned before are described as containing new information. It contrasts with **given** information.

node: an item whose patterns of co-occurrence with others is under examination. It is usually a word, but may also be a multi-word unit, syntagm, bundle or a single character.

n-gram: a string of words, parts of speech, phonemes, syllables, etc. An n-gram consisting of one item is a unigram, of 2 a bigram of 3 a trigram after which the number is used (e.g. 5-gram). N-grams consisting of word forms are (lexical) bundles, of parts of speech are syntagms, whereas hybrid n-grams and collostructions contain lexical word(s) and parts of speech.

normal distribution: a pattern observed in many datasets where most of the values are close to the average (mean) value, forming a bell-shaped curve when this is plotted on a graph. Many statistical procedures assume normal distribution, but this can be problematic since language data such as word frequencies is typically not normally distributed: see Zipf's law.

normalised frequency: a frequency expressed relative to some other value, as a proportion of the whole, for example, the frequency of a word relative to the total number of words in the corpus. Normalised frequencies can be compared even if they arise from datasets of different sizes.

paradigmatic: concerned with how each word in a text reflects a choice from a number of possible words. Often thought of as the vertical axis of text when viewed in corpora. See also syntagmatic.

parallel corpus: a corpus consisting of the same texts in several languages. This typically means a set of texts written in one language together with each text's translation into a second language or several languages.

parsing: the process of analysing the syntactic structure of a text. By extension, any kind of corpus annotation which indicates syntactic structure.

PARSNIP: topics that are not traditionally welcome in foreign language textbooks form the acronym PARSNIP: Politics, Alcohol, Religion, Sex, Narcotics, -isms, Pork.

participle: a non-finite verbal form, normally one that can function as an adjective. English verbs have two participles; the present participle is used in marking progressive aspect, while the past participle is used in marking perfect aspect and the passive.

particle: a word that has a grammatical function such as *to* marking the infinitive, *by* when it marks the agent in passive voice, the adverbs and prepositions in phrasal verbs, *for* marking the beneficiary in dative constructions.

part-of-speech tagging (POS tagging): the process of adding part-of-speech tags to a text; a form of annotation. Usually undertaken automatically by a tagger program.

part-of-speech tags (POS tags): codes added to each word in a corpus to indicate the grammatical category of that word (e.g. noun, verb, adjective, etc.).

passive: one of two voices in English, this is a grammatical construction where the normal arguments of a verb are rearranged: the direct object becomes the subject, and the subject is demoted to an optional adjunct. It is formed with the auxiliary *be* and the past participle, and the demoted subject is marked with the preposition *by*, e.g. *These shoes were made by a cobbler*. The non-passive voice is the **active**.

patterns of normal usage: observing words and phrases in multiple contexts indicates the great extent to which a language is patterned. When we hear or read a word, we predict what comes next. We are able to do this because of our vast exposure to words through which we are primed for co-occurrences (Hoey 2005), and also due to our knowledge of the world as captured in schema (see for example, the Frame Semantics of Fillmore). Some of the items in this glossary are patterns of normal usage, e.g. collocation, word templates.

perfect aspect: in English, the perfect aspect is a grammatical category applied to verbs, indicating a completed event; it is formed from the auxiliary *have* followed by a past participle, e.g. *This boy has studied at film school.*

periphrasis: the use of separate words instead of inflections to express a grammatical relationship.

permalink: pages in online databases have very long, albeit meaningful URLs that are often archived and difficult to find again at a later date. A permalink is a human-readable URL that redirects to these full URLs. Sketch Engine has implemented a permalink system which reduces a URL of hundreds of characters to about ten. They begin, http://ske.li/.

post-modification: elements in a noun phrase that modify the head noun and follow it: in English, relative clauses and preposition phrases.

predicate: in the grammatical analysis of a clause, the predicate is the whole of the clause except the subject, i.e. it includes the verb and any other noun phrases or other constituents.

pre-modification: elements in a noun phrase that modify the noun and precede it, such as other nouns, adjectives or genitive noun phrases, e.g. *proven track record of games sales*.

present participial clauses: in English, subordinate clauses centred around a present participle whose implied subject is the same as the main clause they are linked to, e.g. *They thought long and hard about it, drifting through possibles.*

priming: Lexical Priming theory suggests that we are primed, i.e. readied through a lifetime of experience with words, to expect them to be in the company of other words, their collocations, and to expect words to appear in certain grammatical situations, their grammatical colligations, and in certain positions in text and discourse, their textual colligations. From another perspective, grammar is the product of the accumulation of all the lexical primings of an individual's lifetime. As we collect and associate collocational primings, we create semantic associations and colligations.

proform: a pro-form is a type of function word or expression that expresses the same content as another word, phrase, clause or sentence where the meaning is recoverable from the context. For example, pronouns and the verb *do* in *Yes I did.*

progressive aspect: an aspect in English which indicates an event that is ongoing and not bounded in time. It is formed with auxiliary *be* followed by the present participle, for example, *Maybe he was imagining a life with the woman in the movie.*

qualitative analysis: an analysis that does not rely on numeric data. For example, if you look at a word in a concordance and analyse its usage based on your own understanding of the examples you have seen, this is a qualitative analysis.

quantitative analysis: an analysis that is based on statistics, whether basic statistics such as frequency, or more advanced techniques such as significance testing, cluster analysis or factor analysis.

range: the number words or tokens to the left and right of the node

reference corpus: a corpus which contains samples of language that represent its general nature rather than a specific register.

register: a way of classifying texts according to non-linguistic criteria, such as the purpose for which a text was produced, the intended audience, the level of formality, whether its purpose is narration or description and so on. The term genre is also used to mean this.

representativeness: a corpus which is ideally representative is one that contains all the types of text, in the correct proportions, that are needed to make the contents of the corpus an accurate reflection of the whole of the language or variety of language that it samples.

sampling frame: a sampling frame specifies how samples are to be chosen from the population of text, what types of texts are to be chosen, the time they come from and other such features. The number and length of the samples may also be specified.

semantic association: see semantic preference.

semantic prosody: the tendency exhibited by some words or idioms to occur consistently with either positive or negative meanings. It extends over more than one unit and affects the co-selection of lexis.

semantic set: a group of words with a common element of meaning – they can occupy another word's syntactic slot. For example, the set of things that we wear is limited, the set of attributes that public transport has is limited, the set of ways of cooking rice is limited.

semantic tagging: a process of corpus annotation where each word is assigned one or more tags indicating its semantic category, e.g. cognition, or in some cases its semantic relationships to other words.

semantic type: a superordinate for a set of words that can occupy a slot in a grammar pattern or word template, e.g. state of affairs, document.

semi-modal verb: a category of auxiliary verb constructions which are used to mark modality but which do not have all the grammatical features of the nine central modals. Examples are *be going to, have to, want to.*

sexist language: language which most typically uses masculine pronouns for people in general.

speech acts: speaking is doing, e.g. when you say *I promise,* you are promising. Other examples include, *ordering, greeting, warning, inviting* and *congratulating.*

snapshot corpus: a corpus which contains a fixed sample representing a specified form of the language at a specified time; a type of sample corpus: contrasts with monitor corpus.

stance adverb/ial: indicates the attitude of the speaker towards a state-of-affairs. For example, *surprisingly, undoubtedly, contrary to our expectations.*

statistical significance: a quantitative result is considered statistically significant if there is a low probability (usually lower than 5%) that the figures extracted from the data are simply the result of chance. A variety of statistical procedures can be used to test statistical significance.

subjunctive: a verb mood used in the expressions of wishes, hypothesis, doubt, supposition, etc.

synchronic: relating to the study of language or languages as they exist at a particular moment in time, without reference to how they might change over time (compare: diachronic). A synchronic corpus contains texts drawn from a single period - typically the present or very recent past.

synonym: a word which has the same or similar meaning to another. In many cases, only one of the synonyms is appropriate in a certain context.

syntagmatic: relating to the sequential syntactic relationships between units in a linguistic structure. Often thought of as the horizontal axis in corpora.

tagger: a computer program that automatically applies some type of analytic corpus annotation. On its own, the word tagger usually implies a part-of-speech tagger, but lemmatisers and semantic taggers are also types of tagger.

tagging: an informal term for annotation, especially forms of annotation that assign an analysis to every word in a corpus (such as part-of-speech or semantic tagging).

tagset: a set of tags covering all parts of speech. The two most widely used with English corpora are CLAWS and Penn Treebank.

tense: a term used differently in pedagogy and linguistics. A tense to linguists involves morphological change, e.g. *breed/bred, record/recorded* which results in English having two tenses only, namely past and present. The combinations with English's two aspects, perfect and continuous, such as present perfect, past continuous are referred to as tenses in language pedagogy.

text: any artefact containing language usage - typically a written document, e.g. book, periodical, leaflet, sign, webpage, t-shirt slogan, or a recorded and/or transcribed spoken text, e.g. speech, broadcast, conversation.

theoretical linguistics: the branch of linguistics concerned with the structure of language as a system, phonology, morphology, syntax and semantics in particular, and with the different theories that have been proposed regarding the nature of this system.

token: any single, particular instance of an individual word in a text or corpus. Compare: lemma, type.

topic trail: consists of the key words and phrases that represent the topics of a text. Short texts typically have a several topics and the trails most clearly manifest when they are colour-coded in the text itself. This depicts how they interweave through the text. Topic trails cannot be identified by searching corpora although they can be used as rational sets of vocabulary items for further study. Topic Trails are different from Identity chains and similarity chains.

transitive: a transitive verb is one that has both a subject and a direct object. The transitive construction is the grammatical structure, found in many languages, of a clause containing a verb together with its subject and direct object.

t-test: a statistical test used in the calculation of collocations.

type: a word form. Any difference of form makes a word into a different type. One type may occur many times in a text or corpus; all tokens that consist of exactly the same characters are considered to be examples of the same type. See also token, lemma,

type-token ratio: a measure of vocabulary diversity in a corpus, equal to the total number of types divided by the total number of tokens. The closer the ratio is to 1 (or 100%), the more varied the vocabulary is. This statistic is not comparable between corpora of different sizes.

valency: the number of arguments a verb takes is its valency, e.g. transitive verbs have a subject and an object, therefore a valency of two.

WLT (word form, lemma, POS): when a corpus is compiled, every token is placed on a separate line in the database. In most cases, the token is a word form and it is accompanied by its lemma and POS tag. Non-words are mostly punctuation, which is also accompanied by a POS tag. The database listing therefore consists of Word Form + Lemma + POS, hence WLT. This acronym has been created for use in DESKE.

word cloud: this is a visual representation of a text's key words using colour and size. While the colours do not express anything, the size represents the frequency of word forms, not lemmas. Grammar words are excluded because they are held in a stop list, i.e. a preset list of words to exclude.

word family: word family refers to sets of words that form through morphological process of inflection and word formation. For example, intense: *intensely, intenseness, intensification, intensified, intensifies, intensify, intensifying, intensity, intensive, intensively*. In some pedagogical literature, however, word family refers to a set of topic-based words, e.g. sister, mother, daughter, aunt – see lexical set.

word form: the five word forms of the lemma *go* are *go, goes, going, went, gone*. Adjective word forms include *good, better, best* and nouns *computer, computers* and *datum, data*.

word profile: a set of short, indicative sentences expressing the real world relationships between a headword and its collocates. Cumulatively, they amount to a description of the item. Originally termed *cognitive profile* by Hanks.

word template: a word and the semantic sets of its collocates within its colligation patterns arranged in unmarked word order.

Zipf's law: the frequency of any word in a corpus is inversely proportional to its rank in a frequency table. Thus the most frequent word will occur approximately twice as often as the second most frequent word, which occurs twice as often as the fourth most frequent word, etc.

Answer Key

Introduction

1. What does "affordance" mean? the multiple learning opportunities that a text offers.
2. What is attested language? language that has been produced as a genuine communicative act.
3. What is core language? it is a subset of a language that contains the elements that all idiolects and dialects have in common.
4. What is lexicogrammar? All of the options provided.
5. How do contemporary dictionaries differ from older ones? Modern dictionaries contain information about grammar as well as vocabulary.
6. What is Sketch Engine? SKE is a tool used by applied linguists to explore language.
7. Which contexts do words occur in? all of the options provided.
8. Does a reference corpus aim to represent everything it can about a language? Yes.
9. What is an armchair linguist? linguists who rely on intuition.
10. Where do our idiolects come from? all of the options provided.
11. Who cleans up the language in corpora so that there are no mistakes or taboo language? Nobody cleans it up.
12. Why aren't corpora commonly used in language classrooms? all of the options provided.
13. Why is fuzziness important in language study? all of the options provided.
14. What higher order thinking skills are involved in corpus use by language learners? all of the options provided.

Chapter 1

Language

1. What company does *kick the bucket* keep in the BNC? die.
2. The collocation *handsome woman* is used to describe a certain type of woman in modern English. True.
3. What is the modern English equivalent of *doth*? does.
4. Is *why* followed by both *can't* and *cannot*? *why can't* is standard, but *why cannot* is rare
5. When someone is *in cahoots with* someone, ... they are doing something bad together.
6. Is it true that the collocation *fall pregnant* means that someone became pregnant unintentionally and now regrets it. No.

Linguistics

1. Why are corpus finds normalised? so that findings can be compared across various corpora
2. Deviations from the normal, standard, typical way of doing something are said to be …. a marked choice.
3. Match the terms with their definitions

polysemy	when a word has several meanings
troponym	a verb which is a sub-type of another superordinate verb
hyponym	a word which is at a lower semantic level
co-hyponym	words which are sub of the same superordinate
hypernym	a word which is at a higher semantic level

4. Why is a corpus more suitable for language study than the whole internet? all of these reasons.
5. What does *grammaticality* refer to? an intuitive judgement about the accuracy of a sentence

Chapter 2

There are no quiz questions for this chapter.

Chapter 3

Language

1. Does the verb *hamper* appear to have positive or negative prosody? negative.
2. In the BNC, which use of *bound to* is the most frequent? as a modal verb.
3. Which use of *given that* is anaphoric? *that* is stressed in speech and marked with a comma in writing.
4. I thought *lend* was the verb and *loan* was the noun. Which statement accords with your corpus findings? both are used as verbs with similar normalised frequencies in the BNC and in ETT
5. Which collocations in Q 79 make positive semantic prosody? *avid, dulcet*

Linguistics

1. Which one of these features are true of copular verbs? instead of objects, they have complements.
2. Does Penn Treebank distinguish between *to* as a preposition and as a particle marking the infinitive? Yes.
3. Which statement about collocation and colligation is **not** correct? before 1957 when Firth published his work on collocation and colligation, speakers used language in a much more random way
4. Why do frequency graphs almost always show that some findings are very frequent, with other results becoming less and less frequent? Zipf's law.

Chapter 4

1. What is the node word of the word cloud on p.71? Versatile.
2. Which one of these is **not** true of a thesaurus? entries are arranged in alphabetical order.
3. What is an and/or relationship? when pairs of words are joined by either *and* or *or*.

4. Which definition of *phrase* given corresponds to Sketch Engine's Phrase field? a string of word forms.
5. What term is used for spoken sentences? utterance.

Chapter 5

Language

1. Do the frequencies of the words in the word family of *advantage* demonstrate Zipfian tendencies? Yes.
2. Which one of these features of a word can you **not** reliably infer from meeting it once in context? meaning.
3. Match the verbs on the left with their objects.

    shoulder   burden
    toe   line
    stomach   idea
    thumb   ride
    knuckle   (no object)

4. Which one of these verbs collocates with eggshells and carefully? tread.
5. Which is the most frequent wording of the most frequent finding in Q103? Do you know what I mean.
6. What semantic prosody emerges when the phrase *or just plain* is used? clearly negative.
7. What can be inferred about the meaning and/or use of *slouch* (noun)? people are not usually describe as "a slouch", only "no slouch".
8. Which of the forms of perfect are formed with *have*? all of the options provided.
9. Match these nouns with their types.

    freedom, perseverance, talent   abstract
    rain, penchant, zodiac, motherland, ethos   singular
    jury, minority, headquarters, mafia   collective
    yeast, lager, muslin, lava, lipstick   mass
    advice, progress, work, hair, rice   uncountable

10. What semantic prosody emerges when *amid* is used? somewhat negative.

Linguistics

1. Match these terms with their glosses.

    lemma   head word for a set of inflections which has the same meaning
    lexeme   a word or multi-word unit that expresses a single meaning
    morpheme   the smallest unit that expresses meaning
    conversion   the change of part of speech of a word without inflection
    word formation   a process that creates new meanings

2. Which term is different from the other three? polysemy.
3. Is it unusual for phrasal verbs to be polyemous? No.

4. What do polysemy and homonymy always have in common? the word has the same spelling regardless of meanings.
5. Based on BNC data, would you recommend using capital letters after semicolons? No.
6. Which of these features are expressed periphrastically in English? using auxiliary verbs to form aspect.
7. How is the sentence stem, *having said that*, used? to warn the listener that the next piece of info presents a different perspective.

Chapter 6

Language

1. Which pronoun is used for non-sexist 3rd person singular reference? their.
2. Which one of these things is not described as *positively dangerous* in the BNC? weather
3. Which of the following qualify as delexical verbs? take a bath.
4. There are not very many adjectives between *give* and *nod*: what do they express? the nod didn't take long.

Linguistics

1. What does Hanks mean by *meaning potential*? of the several meanings a word might have, it is the context which realises or actualises the meaning.
2. What are word association lists? all of the options provided.
2. Are word association lists another way of deriving collocation lists? No.
4. How is *positively + adj* usually used? as a predicate.
5. What is a "light" verb? a verb that doesn't carry much meaning.
6. Bundles are more closely associated with M language than O language (in LUG terms). False.
7. Which of the following are features of bundles? None of these.
8. Which parts of speech have patterns in the COBUILD sense? verbs and nouns and adjectives.
9. In the patterns of verbs, which one does not include the subject of the verb? COBUILD patterns.
10. Observing vocabulary in word templates teaches a word's typical company. True.
11. What can grammatizing a word template involve? all of the options provided.
12. How do word templates teach syntax? their elements are presented in unmarked word order.

Chapter 7

Language

1. Which novel starts "It is a truth universally acknowledged ..."? Pride and Prejudice (Austen).
2. Somebody *proves* something. Really? this use of *prove* is quite rare.
3. Which varieties of English use *the high street*? UK.
4. Marriage equality: the collocates of same-sex marriage are mostly ... legal.
5. Regional variation: Match these three words representing the same entity with their variety of English.

    footpath   Australia

Answer Key 121

> sidewalk   America
> pavement   Britain

6. What word is far more frequent at the beginning of spoken sentences or utterances than in written ones? I.

Linguistics

1. What is meant by "primed idiolect"? the linguistic resources that each individual has is a result of their long-term exposure to language.
2. Which of the following statements are true of David Lee's Classification (DLC)? DLC is more fine-grained than the BNC's own text classification.
3. Which part of speech most frequently follows *prove*? Adjective.
4. Which of the following represent deixis? all of the options provided.
5. Building the Brown Corpus was considered a waste of time and money, because ... it was claimed that native speakers have enough intuition to answer questions
6. How is the sentence stem, *having said that*, used? to warn the listener that the next piece of info presents a different perspective.

Chapter 8

Language

1. Adverbs ending in -ly tend to be ... all of the options provided.
2. Words ending in f ... some of the above is true sometimes.
3. Is *themself* used in both spoken and written language, in the BNC? mostly spoken.
4. Verbs following prepositions always use the –ing form. False.
5. Is the structure NOUN of NOUN relatively more frequent in ... informative texts.
6. What do the two spellings, *blond* and *blonde*, indicate? gender.

Linguistics

1. Syntagms consist of ... parts of speech and function words.
2. Do question tags always contain contractions? mostly.
3. What does lempos mean? lemma + part of speech.
4. Would you say that less frequent verbs of saying are semantically richer? Yes.
5. Which of these points is not true of the mandative subjunctive? It is only used in written language.

Chapter 9

Language & Linguistics

1. What type of corpus has translated texts as well as the source language? parallel.
2. English, Czech, German and Italian are the only languages available in the Opus suite? False.
3. Is the Opus suite of corpora the only parallel ones available in SKE? No.
4. Does *galore* have a positive or negative prosody? positive.
5. Hypernym-hyponym relationships are quite consistent across languages and relatively easy to

translate. False.

Chapter 10

Language

1. Is *to spill ink* a ... idiom.
2. What things do we *clench*? buttocks, fist and jaw.
3. In a list of collocates of *naked* in the BNC, which types of nouns are most common? parts of the body, e.g. *breast, torso.*
4. Is *naked eye* a ... idiom.
5. What do the -ly adverbs collocating with the verb peer tell us? peering is not something you do for fun

Linguistics

1. Is a verb + preposition e.g. decide between, a collocation or a colligation? colligation.
2. Are word association lists another way of deriving collocation lists? No.
3. What is a lexeme? a unit of meaning.
4. How many words are in a two lexeme collocation? at least 2.
5. Which of the following are considered collocations, as espoused in DESKE? none of these.
6. Are collocates useful when inferring the meaning of an unknown lexeme? quite useful.
7. A collocation list sorted by T-score mostly has at the top ... function words.
8. Mutual Information listings contain words that are ... rare in the corpus but common with the node word.
9. LogDice collocation listings ... all of the options provided.
10. What is meant by co-selection? When producing language, ... all of the options provided.

Chapter 11

Language

1. What are the objects of *allay*? fear.
2.   What preposition is most frequent after the chunk that emerges? *on.*
3. What things are people *responsible for*? mainly abstract nouns.
4. Which of these do not follow the intransitive phrasal verb *stand around*? object.
5. Is the phrasal verb stand around separable? No.

Linguistics

1. Which of the following options in word sketches can make them learner friendly? all of the options provided.
2. Which part of speech carries most of the meaning of a text, is most frequent in a text and in the language at large, as well as being the most open to new coinages? Noun.
3. What role does English word order play in determining grammatical relationships? all of the options provided.
4. The words which are semantically richer in a word sketch are at the top of the lists when sorted

by ... score.
5. What is the result of clustering a word sketch? words which are semantically related are grouped.
6. How much more frequent is *symptom* as a plural noun than as a singular noun? six times as frequent.
7. How do word sketches indicate the grammatical relationships between the node and its collocates? by grouping the collocates according to the relationship.
8. Are predicative adjective structures only used with copular verbs? Yes.
9. When used in discourse, which type of adjective provides new information about its noun? predicative.
10. Why is the and/or relationship worth observing? it is not random.
11. Which parts of speech have bound prepositions? verbs and nouns and adjectives.
12. What information about a word does its word template contain? all of the options provided.
13. In cognitive profiles, the collocates can be ... verbs and adjectives and nouns.
14. What does a word template not express? all of the options provided.
15. Which parts of speech can have word templates? all of the options provided.

Chapter 12

Language & Linguistics

1. Which gramrels have no content for *interested* in Sketch Diffs in the BNC? followed by the preposition *in*.
2. In the *interested/interesting* Sketch Diffs in the BNC, there is one column that has plenty of red and green but no white collocates. attributive adjectives.
3. Do *hand* and *hands* occur in the BNC in similar numbers? Yes.
4. Judging by the colours in the *hand/hands* Sketch Diff, the two word forms are used ... quite differently.
5. The Sketch-Diff of student and pupil contains many "white words". What does this indicate? they are semantically similar enough to have many collocates in common.

Chapter 13

Language & Linguistics

1. Match these corpora with the part of speech tag that is most frequent in them.
    NN   BNC Written subcorpus
    PP   LEC
    SENT   CHILDES
2. An n-gram of words creates ... lexical bundles
3. How many of the documents in the BNC are emails? 7
4. Which nouns occur approximately 1,000 times as lemmas in the London English Corpus? *person, course, job, football*

Discussion slips

Slip swapping involves each student having a slip of paper with one question on it. All of the students stand in an area where they can mill around. In pairs, one student asks the other the question on the slip and then they discuss it. They then do the same with the other student's question. When the pair has finished their brief chat, they swap their slips and each one finds a new partner. Since all the pairs are discussing their questions at the same time, all students are interacting the whole time.

During this milling, the teacher circulates, monitors offering help, suggestions, etc. as necessary.

This activity works best with groups of ten or more. In fact, there are ten questions per chapter, so with larger groups, it is necessary to make several copies of the same set, unless previously used slips are slipped in for revision.

DESKE Introduction

What does "affordance" mean?

What is attested language?

What is core language?

What is lexicogrammar?

What is Sketch Engine?

Which contexts do words occur in?

What is an armchair linguist?

Who cleans up the language in corpora so that there are no mistakes or taboo language?

Why aren't corpora commonly used in language classrooms?

What higher order thinking skills are involved in corpus use by language learners?

DESKE Ch. 1

✂ -

Does a reference corpus aim to represent everything about a language?

✂ -

Where do our idiolects come from?

✂ -

Why is fuzziness important in language study?

✂ -

Why are corpus finds normalised?

✂ -

Deviations from the normal, standard, typical way of doing something are said to be ....

✂ -

What does grammaticality refer to?

✂ -

Why is a corpus more suitable for language study than the whole internet?

✂ -

What do you think Kilgarriff meant when he said Language is never ever, ever, random? What is its significance to language teaching and learning?

✂ -

When might you use *curiouser* instead of *more curious*?

✂ -

How do spelling mistakes get into corpora? How should corpus-users deal with them?

DESKE Ch. 3

Which element(s) in the Hierarchy of Language is not included in grammar?

What are the levels in the Hierarchy of Language?

What is the difference between inferring meaning in a text and inferring meaning in a corpus?

Is it true that the collocation *fall pregnant* means that someone became pregnant unintentionally and now regrets it.

When someone is *in cahoots with* someone, ...

In the BNC, which use of *bound to* is the most frequent?

Do collocations occur within the same sentence?

Does *at all* reinforce both positive and negative things? And where in the sentence is it typically found?

According to everyone, *according to me* is wrong. Is it? According to whom?

Describe several steps you to to take ownership of your concordance page? What difference do they make to the data you observe.

DESKE Ch. 4

What is an and/or relationship?

What term is used for spoken sentences?

What role does English word order play in determining grammatical relationships?

Which part of speech carries most of the meaning of a text, is most frequent in a text and in the language at large, as well as being the most open to new coinages?

What is a word cloud?

What is a *pattern*, in linguistic terms?

What are the distinguishing features of word clouds?

Which words do and do not appear in a word cloud?

Which words are included in a thesaurus list or word cloud?

Who was Peter Roget?

DESKE Ch. 5

What is M language and O language according to Linear Unit Grammar?

What did you find out about the use of numbers at the beginning of sentences? (Q138)

How does knowing a word family thoroughly contribute to fluency? Can you think of any examples? Give some thought to what contributes to dysfluency.

How can a word family be derived from a corpus?

How much information typically appears in brackets (parentheses)?

According to BNC data, how early did people have email addresses? How is the at symbol (@) used when not in email addresses?

Why do people say things like *not uninteresting*? Is it not enough to say *is interesting*?

Is it true that past participles are only used in compound forms?

A multi-word unit is used for a single word in another language. Would you say that the need for an MWU indicates a lexical gap?

How is the asterisk used in searching?

DESKE Ch. 6

✂ -

What does Hanks mean by *meaning potential*?

✂ -

What are word association lists?

✂ -

Which nominative/subject pronoun is used for non-gender specific 3rd person singular reference?

✂ -

How long has *their/them* been used as non-sexist 3rd person singular reference?

✂ -

What is a "light" verb?

✂ -

Observing vocabulary in word templates teaches a word's typical company. Discuss.

✂ -

What can grammatizing a word template involve?

✂ -

How do word templates teach syntax?

✂ -

Are you aware of any lexical gaps in English? For example, there may be words in your mother tongue which do not have equivalents in English.

✂ -

What are some features of delexical verbs?

DESKE Ch. 7

What is meant by "primed idiolect"?

Somebody *proves* something. Really? Discuss

Building the Brown Corpus was considered a waste of time and money, because ...

Can you envisage any use for diachronic corpus findings in foreign language education?

What word is far more frequent at the beginning of spoken sentences or utterances than in written ones?

Is it true that above-mentioned and aforementioned are used in written and spoken language respectively?

Ubiquitous looks like a rather specialised word. Is it?

Do men say *sorry* more than women?

How are text types allocated to texts crawled from the internet in large corpora?

What text types are in the BNC?

DESKE Ch. 8

✂ -

Do question tags always contain contractions?

✂ -

Adverbs ending in -ly tend to be ...

✂ -

What is serendipity? Can you think of any examples in your life in general, or your linguistic life?

✂ -

Is *themself* used in both spoken and written language, as represented in the BNC?

✂ -

What do the two spellings, *blond* and *blonde*, indicate?

✂ -

Is *which* always preceded by a comma?

✂ -

Who or whom? Discuss.

✂ -

Which words trigger the mandative subjunctive?

✂ -

When don't you need to use square brackets in CQL queries?

✂ -

How do you search for punctuation in CQL queries?

DESKE Ch. 9

What type of corpus has translated texts as well as the source language?

Can you suggest any approaches to using parallel corpora in language teaching? Do any caveats come to mind?

Is the Opus suite of corpora the only parallel ones available in SKE?

Hypernym-hyponym relationships are quite consistent across languages and relatively easy to translate.

Do translated words have the same connotations and/or semantic prosody that they have in English?

Is this figure of speech, litotes, peculiar to English?

How do question tags manifest in translations in other languages that you know?

Is it possible to search in more than two languages at at time?

Is it possible to create a CQL query when using parallel corpora in Sketch Engine?

Have you found any equivalents of lexical gaps in pairs of languages?

DESKE Ch. 10

✂ -

Are word association lists another way of deriving collocation lists?

✂ -

What is a lexeme?

✂ -

How many words are in a two lexeme collocation (TLC)?

✂ -

Are collocates useful when inferring the meaning of an unknown lexeme?

✂ -

Mutual Information listings contain words that are ...

✂ -

How and why might language teachers use the Hoey Procedure?

✂ -

What is meant by co-selection? When producing language, ...

✂ -

Do compound nouns have verb and adjective collocates?

✂ -

When a word is polysemous, what activates its meanings in context?

✂ -

Does lexical support manifest across texts, or hover around certain words?

DESKE Ch. 11

How do word sketches indicate the grammatical relationships between the node and its collocates?

When used in discourse, which type of adjective provides new information about its noun?

Why is the *and/or* relationship worth observing?

Which parts of speech have bound prepositions?

What use is clustering a word sketch? What observations can be made?

In cognitive profiles, which parts of speech can the collocates be?

The Sketch diff of *interested/interesting* is a gold mine of data about this word. How might you use some of it to teach this often confused/confusing pair of adjectives to B2 students?

What do you notice about the constructions in cognitive profiles?

Is distinguishing the objects of verbs enough to disambiguate them?

How can word sketch data be employed in the teaching of prepositions?

DESKE Ch. 13

✂ -

An n-gram of **words** creates ...

✂ -

Why do think that so many of the most frequent 4-word bundles in the BNC's fiction subcorpus contain *n't*?

✂ -

In what situations might language teachers use some of the word list functions?

✂ -

How many hapax legomena are there in a corpus?

✂ -

Are words with the feminine suffix, -ess, fading from use?

✂ -

How new and how frequent is the question tag, *innit*?

✂ -

What does the two lexeme collocation (TLC) definition of collocation include and exclude?

✂ -

What are the essential differences between semantic prosody and connotation?

✂ -

What can be learnt about first language acquisition from corpora?

✂ -

How and why are white lists used in the Word List tool?